VGM Opportunities Series

OPPORTUNITIES IN
TRUCKING CAREERS

Ken Scharnberg

Foreword by
Thomas J. Donohue
Former President and CEO
American Trucking Associations

 **VGM Career Horizons**
NTC/Contemporary Publishing Group

Library of Congress Cataloging-in-Publication Data
Scharnberg, Ken, 1947–
    Opportunities in trucking careers / Ken Scharnberg. — Rev. ed.
       p.   cm. — (VGM opportunities series)
    ISBN 0-8442-6363-X (cloth). —ISBN 0-8442-6364-8 (pbk.)
    1. Trucking—Vocational guidance—United States. I. Title.
  II. Series.
  HE5623.S32   1999
  388.3'24'0973—dc21   98-42987
                                          CIP

Cover Photo Credits:
Top left, top right, and bottom right, UniGroup, Inc., Fenton, Missouri;
bottom left, courtesy Consolidated Freightways, Menlo Park, California.

CONTENTS

Lure of the open road. Industry origins. The modern trucking industry.

Life on the road. Education and training. Qualifications. Earnings. Trucking career advantages.

Hauling freight. Refrigerated transport. Flatbed operations. Household movers. Liquid bulk operations. Hauling livestock. Multiple trailers. The local driver. The construction driver.

Mileage and bonuses. Team drivers. Percentage compensation. Contract drivers. Owner/operators. Let the driver beware.

ABOUT THE AUTHOR

Ken Scharnberg has accrued in excess of 2 million accident-free miles during a 18-year career in the trucking business. He has held various positions in the trucking industry: driver, lease operator, owner/operator, operations manager, fleet manager, and agency manager.

Mr. Scharnberg, a graduate of Concordia Teachers' College, has written and sold over 400 articles and stories, most dealing with the trucking industry. He recently resigned as veterans affairs editor after seven years at *The American Legion Magazine.* His former positions include being bureau chief for *Business Journal of West Texas,* editor of the *Martin County News,* copywriter for Nebe Communications, editor-at-large for Go West Trucking Management, and Midwest correspondent for *American Trucker Magazine.*

Scharnberg currently lives in Iowa, where he writes full time and occasionally works as a casual driver for various carriers.

FOREWORD

To embark on a career in trucking is to join the industry that moves America. Everything you use—this book, the morning newspaper, the food on your table, the clothes on your back, and the medicine you take when you're sick—was brought to you by truck.

The trucking industry carries 74 percent of all manufactured goods and makes up 78 percent of the nation's freight bill. Trucks are on the road 24 hours a day, every day of the year, carrying the freight that America's businesses and consumers need.

When you consider a career in trucking, you are in good company. There are about 362,000 companies in the United States that operate trucks. In total, the industry employs 8.5 million people—more than 2.9 million of whom are truck drivers.

The trucking industry today is facing a serious shortage of qualified men and women—especially drivers. Consequently, wages and benefits are improving. And great progress has been made to bring improved technology and higher safety standards to the industry. We need qualified, safety-conscious professionals who are committed to the on-time, safe delivery of our nation's goods.

New industry standards for improved logistics and the quick movement of freight mean even more opportunities. Electronic data interchange, just-in-time delivery systems, "intelligent" highway systems—these are the growing technologies which will challenge us and require bright, energetic people to test, develop, and expand them.

The trucking industry is not just about moving freight— it's about being a part of an increasingly sophisticated logistics system that will keep America competitive.

If you have what it takes—if you want to contribute to an industry with boundless opportunities—we want you. In return, you can find a rewarding career as you set forth on the ride of your life.

Thomas J. Donohue
Former President and CEO
American Trucking Associations

PREFACE

I first climbed behind the wheel of a truck in 1973. Green, inexperienced, untrained and ignorant, it was miraculous I didn't pile that rig up within the first five miles of the terminal, but somehow I muddled through and over the years amassed a respectable number of miles—over 2 million— and so far, have avoided any accidents. Well, almost.

When I allowed my driver's license to lapse, I was forced to retake my driving test and yes, bumped a parked car while backing up. There was no damage done, no insurance claim filed, but it was certainly an awkward moment, since Amy, the Department of Transportation examiner, was sitting right there beside me. She looked at me, I looked at her, she just smiled faintly, and drew a large "X" across the exam sheet. Three days later, shaken and considerably more humble, I did manage to renew my license. That was in May of 1997.

Between my first experience and that fateful exam, the changes that have taken place have been both glaring and subtle. In 1973, there were almost no women behind the wheel of the big rigs. In 1975, when I married, my wife was one of the first females to ply the nation's highways as part of a team. Have some of the problems that we faced disappeared? Well,

I no longer have to stand guard at the doorway of a community shower in a truckstop while my wife showers and blow dries her hair. Today, female truck drivers are as common as bugs on the windshield.

It wasn't until 1977 that I finally got a truck with power steering and 1984 before I had a rig with an air conditioner— which only worked about two months—and 1988 when my wife and I finally had a double sleeper rig that allowed both of us to sleep in uncramped comfort.

The point, of course, is that the trucking industry is fluid; it never stands still. What is true and accurate today will almost certainly change tomorrow. When I began my career, the interstate system was not even wholly built. Runaway trucks on mountain grades were common and big money for a skilled driver was 12-cents a mile, while serious money for a trucking executive was about $12,000 a year.

Overall, I'm very proud of the industry. When female drivers and safety personnel finally did break into the business, there was none of this nonsense that has been so common in other industries. If experienced drivers earned 32-cents a mile, it does not matter whether the driver is male, female, black, white, Hispanic, or Asian. While glass ceilings may still exist in isolated instances administratively, the backbone of the industry—the driver—is treated as an equal.

Trucking as a career? For those who can tolerate it, it is terrific, but be warned: Caution. In some cases, trucking may be addictive; a habit impossible to kick.

Hope you find *Opportunities in Trucking Careers* useful.

Ken Scharnberg

CHAPTER 1

FIRST THERE WAS FREIGHT

Imagine driving a four-cylinder, 40-horse truck whose engine is connected to the rear end by something that looked like a bicycle chain. There is no enclosed cab, no heater, certainly no air conditioner, and bundled about your feet is a massive buffalo skin robe, your only connection from the cold or rain. Then picture yourself accompanied by four other people, one to photograph, one to act as a mechanic, and two more to assist in engineering at the point where the road ends. Now imagine pitching a tent each night, traveling down roads that were little more than horse paths, literally building crude, shaky bridges to enable your vehicle to cross gullies and canyons, climbing the Rockies up trails that are narrower than your vehicle is wide, then coming down those same mountains in a vehicle whose only brakes are a series of steel bands around the drive shaft, and doing all this for a publicity stunt for a soap company.

Sound pretty far-fetched? This describes the first officially recorded cross-country truck haul in the United States.

Times have changed and with them, the trucking industry.

LURE OF THE OPEN ROAD

The excitement, romance, respect, and adventure of traveling the country's highways in command of one of the mightiest vehicles on the boulevard.

If this is your idea of trucking, you're both right and wrong. In this book, we will address both the occupation of driver and the many affiliated careers available within the trucking industry. As you will soon see, starting a career in trucking isn't a simple matter of getting behind the wheel and hitting the highway. For one thing, as time goes on, more and more employers are demanding an educational background beyond high school.

Most industries, including the trucking industry, are moving away from their simplistic roots into the high-tech environments of modern businesses. For instance, in 1971, very few firms had computers. By 1980, most had at least computerized their payroll. Today, computers perform a myriad of tasks, including sophisticated tracking systems that can pinpoint a truck and load within five hundred feet of its actual geographic location through the use of satellite technologies. Today, most large companies and an increasing number of smaller operations rely on on-board computer/satellite systems for communication, driver check-in, load dispatch, and even log maintenance.

For the job applicant starting out with just a high school diploma, it is increasingly difficult to advance through the ranks in any business, including the transportation industry. Therefore, as you read this book, keep in mind that comments about the education needed for various occupations are intended to reflect minimum requirements, and any training over and above the minimum will make you more attractive to a potential employer.

This chapter offers some background about the business and how it began. At first, you may wonder why you should bother learning how the trucking industry began. That's all just ancient history, right? The answer is that the history of the business follows a logical order and helps explain why careers within transportation often interlink with careers in other fields. In addition, like any business, trucking has its competitors, and in business, it's always a good idea to understand the competition.

The following chapters deal with specific occupations within the industry—what each job is like and what it takes to enter that particular occupation. Two chapters describe being a driver. Driving positions are by far the largest single opportunity within the transportation field. Most experts and trucking associations estimate that 470,000 new drivers will be needed before the turn of the century. However, not everyone is cut out to be a driver, and there are an enormous number of misconceptions concerning the career. The two chapters dedicated to driving will dispel any myths or pre-conceived notions you may have about driving. The first driving chapter highlights some of the requirements and explains how to develop the skills you will need to become a driver. The second chapter looks at the various options that are open to drivers, explains the myriad ways a company might pay a driver, and also lists some of the self-employment opportunities that exist within the industry and are available in few other businesses.

The chapters that follow also address the other occupations within the business. In today's trucking industry, there are dozens of opportunities, and not all of them require that a person spend weeks on end on the highway. The modern truck driver is simply a cog in the wheel of a much larger operation than what regularly meets the eye. From safety to dispatch to sales to logistical planning, it's all part of the trucking industry. Job opportunities range from basic vehicle maintenance to high-tech positions in computer programming and accounting. Perhaps the best news is that the industry is expanding and, because of this, often is willing to train new employees, from drivers to dispatchers. It is indeed an industry of opportunity.

INDUSTRY ORIGINS

Before we look at the business today, let's take a look at how this all began and where it's heading. Trucking, by definition, is the act of moving freight overland from point A to point B, for money. It is, in one form or another, one of the oldest professions. Since people first learned the value of barter or trade, the skill of moving goods of value from one point to another has been increasingly vital. The early Roman emperors recognized the importance of transportation and created the Appian Way, one of the earliest highways in existence. To maintain it, they charged a tariff and, in return, maintained the road and protected the transported goods from bandits. In other words, the Appian Way was an early toll road, and elements of the Roman Legion may be considered the earliest recorded highway patrol.

The first people to hook domestic animals to carts and wagons were called *teamsters,* after the teams of draft animals—usually oxen, horses, or mules—that were used to provide power for the conveyances. In the early days of the North American continent, teamsters hauled everything—from farm produce to explosives—to the farthermost outposts of civilization. (Today, the largest organized union representing truckers still includes the word "teamster" in its name.)

Trucking and the Railroads

Despite its usefulness, animal power does have a few drawbacks. First, even if the animals aren't working, they still must eat. Then, too, they tend to be temperamental, are subject to illness and age, and they are quite limited in the amount of freight they can physically handle. Hence, the first economical intercontinental freight was hauled not by draft animals and teamsters but by the railroad locomotive. The teamsters took the freight from the railhead* and delivered it locally to the receiver, or they hauled products from the shipper to the railhead for cross-country deliveries. Ironically, even as the railways were being built, wagon-loads of supplies and equipment were hauled by freight wagons to the construction points and railheads. In short, the trucking industry helped build its own competition.

The railroads and the trucking industry were destined to become competitors and, for a time, bitter enemies. Today, the railroad industry is declining, with more and more rail

---

*Point on a railroad where trains depart or arrive.

systems being abandoned. Yet, even now, trucking and the railroad industry are interlinked and in this one area, both the rail and trucking industries are growing and expanding. The piggyback system is now a vital and practical means of transport. Loaded freight trailers are loaded onto railcars and hauled to destination points where local trucks hook onto the trailers to make final delivery. Piggyback hauling is an economical system and will continue to expand in the years to come.

Air Freight

The only serious competitor to the trucking business is air freight, which is still a burgeoning "baby" industry. It is worth noting that many of the occupations described in this book exist in other industries, including the air freight business.

Despite competition from air freight companies, the future of trucking is very secure. The increased number of drivers will directly affect related careers within the industry. The greater the demand for trucks and drivers, the greater the demand for affiliated support personnel. And as long as there are consumers, there will be a trucking industry.

THE MODERN TRUCKING INDUSTRY

The birth of the modern trucking industry as we know it took place during World War I when General John "Blackjack" Pershing registered a plea with the auto industry to create a vehicle that could do the work of a mule, but didn't become bogged down, suffer from weather conditions, or require food and water even when not in use. The result was the first of the early trucks. These vehicles were very primitive, little more than automobile chassis outfitted with freight beds. Primitive as they were, few people knew how to operate motor vehicles before 1920. The army arrived at a simple solution. They would train the drivers they needed, drawing upon soldiers already in the military.

Teamsters from the cavalry units were pulled away from their horses and mules and retrained to operate these new-fangled devices. The idea was successful. However, when the war ended, twenty thousand teamsters had learned a new occupation, but found there was no organized industry where they could apply their newly learned trade. Worse still, at war's end, jobs were scarce and unemployment very high. The government had few social service programs, and the GI Bill had not yet been drafted. At the same time, with the war over, the government had little use for the tanks, airplanes, and trucks they had ordered built for the war effort. To raise revenue, the government put this merchandise and equipment up for sale.

Eventually, many drivers bought these surplus trucks from the government after the war, or converted automobiles into freight-hauling trucks, and went into business for themselves. At the same time, enterprising businesspeople recognized the potential in the truck, and they began using trucks and modifying them to meet their own personal business needs. While it may have been a less than auspicious beginning, these ex-GIs and forward-thinking businesspeople set themselves up in business, usually within major cities, to haul freight from piers and rail yards to customers within the area.

One of the problems with the railroad was that rail lines did not run through every community. Towns not serviced by rail faced a major hardship. They had to pay more than merchants and consumers located along the railways to receive manufactured goods, seed, canned goods, and almost everything else. Businesspeople in unserviced areas could not compete with similar businesses located near the railway. It was this situation that gave birth to the trucking industry as a business.

Still, it was a slow beginning. Roads were scarce, and gasoline to power the vehicles was not readily available in every location. Truckers were forced to become mechanics because there were no service stations or repair shops. These early trucks were extremely primitive and subject to mechanical failures. However, as the nation became more mobile, and more and more cars appeared on the scene, demand for a decent road system grew urgent. Along with it, mechanics and repair shops began to appear, and the first of the support industries for trucking came into existence.

At this time, the government faced the overwhelming problem of unemployment. The Great Depression was rapidly destroying the national economy. In order to put a vast number of people to work, a number of major government-sponsored projects were commissioned. One of these projects was a coast-to-coast highway known as Route 66. This project, and the war that was to follow a decade or so later, would combine to legitimatize one of the fastest growing and most vital industries the world would ever witness.

Competition with the Railroad

The trucking industry won both friends and enemies once it started to flourish. One of the most notable enemies was the railroad. They saw their business monopoly threatened, especially when long-established customers curtailed their business with the railroad and began, instead, to ship by truck. Some of the first businesses to do this were the meat-packing companies. The very size of a train car and the fact that it could not stray from its tracks to make delivery in out-of-the-way communities were its biggest drawbacks. Packing plants were not automated, and it took time to fully load a meat car. The car was refrigerated by ice and poorly insulated. Since few customers would or could not accept an entire boxcar of meat at a time, the last customer on the route often ended up with a load of spoiled and worthless merchandise. Though trucks hauled smaller amounts, and were no better insulated at the time than boxcars, their one major advantage was their ability to make direct, immediate deliveries, cutting down on spoilage by a large margin.

FEDERAL LEGISLATION

What had started as a worry for the rail industry now became an all-out war. While railroad lobby groups petitioned Washington to do something about the rapidly expanding trucking industry, railroad workers and their friends physically attacked truckers from time to time in an effort to keep them away or scare them off from potential customers. Railroad workers also tried to strong-arm and threaten some of their own customers to force them to stop doing business with these upstart truckers and continue to use rail service exclusively. It was a bloody and bitter time, with bad feelings developing on both sides of the issue. Congress finally acceded to rail demands and created what we now recognize as the Federal Motor Carriers Act. This act, which outlined safety specifications within the trucking industry and set requirements for drivers and equipment, would eventually create a whole new series of career opportunities within the business. In addition, even though the railroad had hoped to shut down or at least slow the expansion of truck transport, the end result was a much stronger and considerably safer trucking business.

With the Federal Motor Carriers Act came regulation that, in its simplest form, stated that only certain carriers were allowed to haul certain commodities or products within a specified area. These permissions to transport were called "rights," and rights were transferable and marketable.

At the same time, one of the railroad's biggest fears was that trucks, which were capable of delivering freight to any town as long as a road lead to it, would take over the transport business entirely. So the Gateway Laws were created, which probably did more damage to the rail industry than to the trucking industry. The Gateway Laws were a series of legislation designed to ensure that all communities, regardless of size, would be serviced by truck or rail. To accomplish this, the government designed legislation that required trucks, based on their direction of travel, to pass through specific geographic locations. These "gateways" to the East and West were intentionally placed off-route so that direct, straight-line service on long-distance hauls would be impossible. The end result, however, was that industries, which up until then had to locate near a rail line to enable themselves to ship their goods, now began to spring up all over the map, not just along rail lines.

World War II

World War II saw the greatest increase of trucking traffic to date and helped cool the heated, bitter competition between the railroad and the trucking business. Munitions, food, supplies, and equipment moved from all points of the country by truck. As military manufacturers and military bases sprang up, demand for trucking services and for more and better roads increased dramatically. Truckstops—service facilities for trucks and drivers—sprang up overnight. Related industries blossomed. And more and more new jobs were created within the industry to match the ever-increasing demands. As critical wartime materials became increasingly important, trucks began to travel both day and night, and the service station businesses began to cater to these red-eyed, long-haul drivers by creating all-night service areas. The first of the truckstops was born, and even Hollywood got into the act, glamorizing and immortalizing the hard-bitten, tough knight of the highway, the American trucker.

THE INTERSTATE

One of the major, lasting results of the war, and the problems the nation faced with transporting war materials, was the creation of the interstate highway system. The original name for the series of interconnecting multilane highways was the National Defense Highway System. Today, most people simply call them the interstates. These ultramodern roads were designed to be high-speed highways which, in time of war, could be dedicated to transporting loads weighing more than a hundred thousand pounds across the country in the fastest way possible. In peacetime, these highways would answer the country's ravenous demand for a safe, fast highway system. They also gave trucks the final ingredient to become an indispensable industry within the transportation field: the ability to move from point A to point B in a rapid, safe, and efficient manner.

Modern Innovations

Since the introduction of the early motorized trucks, many improvements and innovations have taken place. Early trucks were dangerous, and many pioneers of the industry died building the business. It wasn't until after World War II that a decent system for braking was developed. The war years gave birth to dedicated truck manufacturers. Prior to this, the component parts of a truck were usually the same as those found in passenger cars. Tires, brakes, axles, drivetrains, and steering were usually interchangeable with auto systems, even though the truck was hauling far more weight and traveling over much greater distances than a car. Once it became obvious that the trucking industry was here to stay, manufacturers like Mack, Diamond Reo, White, and International Harvester began to build vehicles specifically designed to take the heavy loads and constant operation required by the motor transportation industry.

The hardships and dangers an early trucker faced are hard to imagine today. It was not until the 1940s that heaters became common in truck cabs. Most drivers operating in the mountains, or in winter weather, wore heavy clothing and often great fur lap rugs thrown over their legs. Air brakes, now standard equipment on trucks, were unheard of in the 1940s, and trucks depended on spring-loaded systems that were susceptible to the vagaries of weather and terrain. Even something as common as the sleeper—the compartment behind the cab designed to be used as a bed—was nonexistent in the early days. And when sleepers were first introduced, they were not always placed immediately behind the cab as they are today. One version, commonly referred to by drivers as the "suicide sleeper," was actually located beneath and behind the driver's compartment, a position that often proved fatal in the event of a collision. The device earned its grim nickname in more than one accident. The early truckers were hardy souls who rivaled the American cowboy's reputation for independence and toughness.

Other milestones in the development of the industry include the diesel engine, which did not become common until the 1950s; the fifth wheel, which is the flat, locking plate that the kingpin in the nose of the trailer attaches to and rides upon; and air brakes.

Another important development happened within the past two decades, when women started to appear behind the wheels of the "big rigs." This was totally unheard of, and when it first began, it caused more than one raised eyebrow. But, today, women have proved their worth, and it is common to find a woman behind the wheel. The trucking industry is actively recruiting women, exploiting what, to them, is an entirely new labor pool. And why not? What other industry can offer starting wages in excess of $30,000 a year, regardless of gender?

Trucking is still in its youth. Today, satellite communication, electronic developments, aerodynamics, and other disciplines are adding more and more to what was once a reasonably simple field. Trucking also happens to be one of the most exciting businesses a person can enter. It has a proud history, and the future looks brighter than ever.

CHAPTER 2

THE PERSON BEHIND THE WHEEL

By far the largest and most visible employment opportunity within the trucking business is being a driver. Everyone has seen truckers rolling up and down the nation's highways, hauling their loads at all hours of the day and night. Hollywood has made movies about them, and television producers have created series about them, but the silver screen depiction of the truck driver is, to put it mildly, a bit distorted.

LIFE ON THE ROAD

To begin with, let's pop a few bubbles created by rumor, Hollywood, and highway "cowboys." The hard, cold truth of the matter is that fewer than six out of ten new drivers last more than a month. Most quit within the first four weeks on the road. This statistic is astounding when you consider that many of those who quit paid up to four thousand dollars to learn how to drive a truck, spent up to six months in a training school, and probably gave up another job to become a driver.

One reason for the alarming rate of turnover among new drivers is that many potential drivers base their career decisions primarily on misinformation. The image of the driver roaring down the road in a big, shiny diesel, sightseeing like a permanent highway tourist is ingrained in the American imagination. While it is true that a road driver sees a lot of the country, what's not immediately obvious is what he or she has given up to do this. Believe it or not, most drivers quit because they have never before experienced the loneliness of the highway—what it is like to be away from the house, from your family and friends, away from all the activities you are used to participating in—in exchange for a career as a truck driver. For lack of a better term, call it homesickness.

Now, before you snicker or laugh, take a good look in the mirror, and ask yourself a few questions. What are your favorite activities? Do you like playing softball on the church or community league? Forget it. Do you enjoy seeing the newly released movies as they come out? Forget it. Do you follow your favorite teams—basketball, baseball, hockey, or whatever—and attend all the home games? Forget it. Have you ever in your life spent two weeks away from home, your family, and friends; returned for a day, then left again for another two weeks; returned for a day, and then left again? That's a true picture of a truck driver's life. In short, truck drivers place their business life ahead of recreation or a scheduled social life. It is certainly not a lifestyle everyone can readily accept or handle. It is an incredibly hard adjustment.

If you are married, or plan to marry, you should know that truck driving—especially long-distance, over-the-road driving—can be one of the most devastating and trying careers on a family and a marriage. Unless you are willing to miss anniversaries, birthdays, family get-togethers, and special events, forget truck driving. The Hollywood image of a trucker—one who's constantly stopping by to see a girlfriend or boyfriend, who's home for the kid's birthday, and makes it back to attend the homecoming game—is, like most things out of Hollywood, a work of fiction.

Perhaps this picture seems too gloomy to be true. Unfortunately, it is an extremely accurate depiction of the life of an over-the-road driver. Trucking firms, who may have half a dozen $160,000 rigs parked out back with no drivers to drive them, may create a different image in their advertising. These companies urgently need to entice drivers to them and have few scruples concerning how they do it. Unfortunately, in their quest for new drivers, some firms resort to rosy advertising or misleading representations.

Yet, there are a great many benefits of a career in truck driving. Before we look at the benefits, let's look at what you need to become a driver.

EDUCATION AND TRAINING

Trucking is special because it is a meaningful occupation that doesn't require a college degree, though many drivers do hold degrees, and a great many work seasonal trucking jobs to earn enough money to attend classes during the winter. (One of the largest employers of this type of seasonal driver is the household moving industry, whose busiest time is from May through August.) Education and training are important to drivers. In the modern trucking business, it takes intelligence to make a living.

It's a timeworn Catch-22, but most companies require that a driver have some experience before they will hire him or her. The obvious question is how do you get experience if no one will hire you? There are two ways. The first, and by far the most common today, is to attend a truck driving school. The second method, common 20 years ago but rapidly disappearing today, is by being hired by an owner/operator and learning the craft from the person who owns the truck. This second method is all but extinct. Tighter and tougher insurance requirements, the rising cost of equipment and repairs, the gradual decline of independents, and the overall risk involved have made the OJT (on-the-job-training) method impractical, dangerous and, in some cases, impossible.

However, as is often the case, when one door closes, another opens. It is becoming increasingly more common for companies—especially the larger carriers such as England, Hunt, Schneider, and others—to offer in-house training for their drivers. In fact, most of these companies require new drivers, even those who have graduated from recognized truck driving schools, to attend their own courses and to make their initial runs with a trainer. With the tendency for bigger, faster, heavier and increasingly complex equipment, expect this trend to expand industry-wide.

Selecting a School

With the current shortage of drivers, truck driving schools are flourishing. Unfortunately, not all schools are created equal, and it pays to be wary when you are shopping for a school. Training, after all, is an important investment in your future, and it is wise to exercise some caution when looking at a vocational truck driver training facility.

To make an intelligent decision, you need to know some basic facts. Let's consider the basic requirements for a driver. The first is age. The law may state that you can hold a commercial or chauffeur's license at age 18 or 19, depending on the state or province where you reside. However, on a practical basis, you will find it extremely difficult, if not impossible, to find a driving job unless you are at least 21. Even then, there are very few companies willing to hire a driver that young. Most will require an age somewhere between 23 and 25.

Moreover, if you are a resident of one of the Canadian provinces, you may find you are required to serve as much as two years in an "apprenticeship" program. In this program you will at first only drive about the yard, then to nearby local destinations, then within a very short range beyond the terminal, then finally, perhaps after two years, over the road.

The reason for this requirement is simple. All carriers must, by law, have insurance coverage to remain in business. All insurers are painfully aware of the statistics on younger drivers. Most insurance companies are unwilling to insure a $120,000 tractor, a $60,000 trailer, and a load that may be worth $500,000 or more and then entrust them to a driver who, statistically, is extremely likely to have an accident behind the wheel.

With these facts in mind, look hard and long at the driving school you are considering. Are they promising to teach you to drive *and* get you a job even though you are only 18? If so, make them prove it before you sign anything, pay anything, or commit to anything. The jobs for the 18- to 21-year-old driver are usually within construction or, in some cases, local delivery services. Few, if any, over-the-road carriers will hire 18-year-olds; as of this writing, no major carriers were absorbing that kind of risk. You may not like it, but this is the hard, cold truth, and it could save you a lot of money and frustration in the long run.

Does accreditation of a school mean anything? The answer here is yes and no. Basically, accreditation is a statement from the state or federal government that says it's okay for the school to be in business. Accreditation is what makes the school eligible for federal and state funding for its students. However, the state or federal government's guarantee that the school is legitimate is not the same as saying it will make a good truck driver out of you.

Today, most schools work in conjunction with one or more carriers, and this is the key to judging the training you are about to receive. Don't be afraid to talk to these carriers or to students who have graduated from the school. Keep in mind if you receive a list of graduates from the school itself, that you are going to receive preselected individuals. No school, or for that matter, no business is going to give you a list of their failures or those who left unhappy with their instruction. The best way to check your potential school is to visit carriers where the school places graduates and fill out the job application, and ask them bluntly, "If I take the course and graduate, will you have a job for me?" Generally, it takes less than 48 hours to "run" an application, check references and driving records, and reach a decision. If the carrier says that they would hire you if you attended the school and passed the course, chances are you've located a legitimate school.

QUALIFICATIONS

What are some of the pitfalls that could prevent you from obtaining employment as a driver? Three areas can shoot you down before you even get started: If you have more than one moving violation in the past year (or past three to five years for many companies), you probably won't qualify; if you have a DWI (driving while intoxicated) conviction, it's 99 percent certain you won't be hired; and if you use illegal drugs, look for another occupation. By law, all companies today require a pre-employment drug test for their drivers, not only prior to employment, but sporadically throughout the year.

In addition, the federal government has a program underway to spot-check drivers for drug and alcohol use at weigh stations and DOT (Department of Transportation) inspection ports across the country. The day of the "pilled-up driver" and the habitual traffic offender is over in the trucking industry. Drug prevention within the transportation industry as a whole—including rail, air, and land transport—has become a priority and mandatory. The drug test has become a standard part of the Department of Transportation physical, and you cannot get a job as a driver without that physical. In addition, more and more companies are becoming self-policing, requiring potential employees to undergo drug testing as an integral part of their own in-house safety program. In other words, if you "do" drugs, you won't drive a truck.

In a further effort to weed out the "outlaw" driver, the federal government has instituted a federal licensing program. At one time, some truckers held operators licenses in a number of states. Since state reporting authorities seldom communicated driving records or offenses to each other, these drivers could effectively hide any tickets they collected by simply producing another driving permit from a different state. The federal licensing system has not only done away with this practice—which has always been illegal—but, in addition, has created a moderately complicated test that all drivers must pass before being commercially licensed.

These stringent requirements have had a major effect within the industry, weeding out a great many drivers who had no business being on the highway. This, in turn, means that even more driving slots are available. Therefore, if you have a squeaky clean driving record, you are attractive to trucking outfits, and you will find yourself very much in demand.

At this point, we should probably address some of the things that are *not* necessary for a career as a truck driver. One major misconception is that you must be some sort of muscle-bound superhero to drive a rig. Today's rigs are deigned for the ease and comfort of the driver. Power steering, air conditioning, climate controls, and many other creature comforts are available in modern rigs, and most companies recognize that the driver's comfort is directly linked to his or her satisfaction with the company and his or her performance on the road. The hardest, most physical acts, excluding loading or unloading, are probably hooking and unhooking trailers. That's not to say physical fitness isn't important for a truck driver, but pure brute strength is seldom necessary to operate a tractor-trailer rig. There are a couple of exceptions, but they are rare and will be addressed later in this book.

The DOT Exam

There is far more to trucking than just learning how to pilot a rig through an obstacle course. In fact, driving may be one of the less challenging topics you address during your training. The federal and state laws governing trucking are myriad and often complicated, and you will be expected to learn those that apply to you and your rig. In fact, before you are allowed to drive a rig, you will have to pass both a physical and a series of written exams. Included in your written exams are a number of licensing requirements. Unlike automobile licenses, a truck driver needs federal certification on his or her license for every conceivable driving situation they might find themselves in. Hence, in addition to a general knowledge test, you will take an exam on air braking systems, may need to take an exam for hazardous material handling, commonly referred to as a HazMat endorsement (which is earned through a written exam), certification for pulling multiple trailers if that is what you intend to do, and another exam for tankers.

In addition, all drivers are required to take a basic Department of Transportation (DOT) written exam each time they enter employment with a carrier. This exam is entirely separate from your driver's license exam. When you complete this test, you will be issued a DOT card stating that you have successfully taken and passed the exam. This, along with your driver's license and your DOT physical card, are almost always asked for when you are stopped at weigh stations or checkpoints by state and federal authorities. You are required by law to have them, and it is illegal for any transportation company to hire you as a driver without them.

The test, while not overly difficult, is fairly thorough. It consists of about four pages of questions covering topics ranging from how many hours a driver can legally log during a 24-hour period to where and when to use flares in case of a breakdown. All questions in the DOT exam are based on information and laws in the Motor Carriers Safety Act. Usually, you can obtain a free copy from any major trucking company or from your public library. A working knowledge of the DOT rules and regulations are vital to your career in the transportation business, even if you don't intend to become a driver.

EARNINGS

Another major misconception about trucking has to do with money. Truck drivers do not, as some advertisements might lead you to believe, make a fortune. You can earn a good living as a driver, but you could earn the same real income from a variety of other occupations, too, and do it without some of the drawbacks inherent in the trucking industry. So that you can judge the economic potential of a trucking career for yourself, let's look at some averages from the "real world" of transportation.

For the moment, we are only going to address the income of the over-the-road driver, or long-distance freight hauler. There are a number of ways to be paid in this business. The most common is by the mile. However, mileage is an elusive thing. Ask any three people how far it is from one point to another, and you will most likely receive three different answers. To avoid discrepancies, the industry adopted a standardized mileage guide many years ago called the *Household Mover's Mileage Guide.* It was the standard of the industry and also the primary basis for payment of truckers. Most refer to these tables and payment rates as "book" miles. This guide is rapidly being replaced by a computer-driven system called the "PC Miler." Both systems suffer from the same drawbacks.

The problem with book miles is that the shortest distance between two points is seldom the same route any sane person would want to take in a 65-foot long, 13-foot high tractor-trailer rig. In short, there is usually a discrepancy between book miles and the actual miles you will travel. Opinions on how large the average margin of error is vary, but most accept it to be between a 10 and 15 percent difference. This may sound unimportant, but when your paycheck is based upon it, it's best to know ahead of time what you are facing. In effect, what you are looking at is being paid for 85 percent of the miles you drive.

Now, let's apply a few real figures to this equation. In an "average" freight operation, each driver logs about 115,000 solo miles a year. At the same time, payment based on book miles is for 97,750 miles. In other words, each driver probably ran 17,250 miles for free during the year. Obviously, the differential between book and actual miles *is* important after all. If you are being paid 31 cents per mile (a fairly common figure), your income will be about $30,302 per year. On the surface, this is a reasonable sum of money, and the opportunity for bigger earnings becomes greater with each passing year, as you become more valuable to the company. Trucking is an industry where raises for experience and expertise are common, a business where it is truly what you know and not who you know.

However, earning figures, even after factoring the book miles into them, are still misleading. Most companies expect you to pay your own way out on the highway. This means meals, personal expenses, and more come out of your pocket. The average cost for the average driver out on the road runs from $22 to $35 per day out, depending on your lifestyle. Again, depending on the company and your route, the amount of time out on the road will vary widely. For argument's sake, assume 22 days per month on the road at $26 per day for 12 months, or a road expense of $6,864 per year. Suddenly, you find that you have a bit more than $23,000 remaining from your income before taxes. So it's easy to see that money is not the primary motivating factor for becoming a driver.

TRUCKING CAREER ADVANTAGES

Why should you choose trucking as your career? Is there anything good about the occupation? The answer, of course, is a resounding "yes." There is an element of freedom involved with trucking. Although you generally call your office each day, you are usually miles away. This gives you a sense of independence seldom awarded an hourly wage employee, or even a salaried executive. For the most part, the company trusts you enough to allow you the independence to operate an expensive piece of equipment, often carrying an expensive load, without direct supervision. They trust you enough to believe you will make delivery on time, that you will get the load in safely, and that you will represent the company to their clients in a courteous and professional manner at both the shipping and receiving ends of your journey. You have proved yourself dependable and trustworthy in their eyes. This factor, in itself, is enough to lead many to join the ranks of drivers traveling the nation's thoroughfares.

Trucking also offers great challenges, and many drivers thrive on that. You are in control of up to eighty thousand pounds of steel and freight and diesel power, expected to operate in light or darkness, good weather and bad. Your judgment and your judgment alone will keep you and your fellow motorists safe and your equipment whole. There is a tremendous sense of pride and accomplishment that comes from meeting this challenge. It's a feeling that must be experienced rather than described.

Trucking also offers job security. While other businesses are laying off workers, there is a very definite shortage of drivers. Once you have proved yourself a capable driver, you will find that the company will do whatever they can, within reason, to keep you on their team and operating happily. This may not translate into huge raises or placing you in a brand new rig each year, but little "perks" are becoming more and more common, from three-day bonus vacations to systems that allow you to take your spouse on the road with you once in a while.

Finally, trucking is an honorable occupation. You can justifiably take pride in making a timely delivery or a safe driving decision. Without trucks and truck drivers, the nation would grind to a halt very quickly. Some say that should all trucks stop making deliveries, the city of New York would run out of food and raw materials within three days. Exaggerated or not, this statistic does give some measure of just how vital the driver's role is in the overall economy of the nation. There simply is nothing else that can take the place of the truck or the truck driver. For those who can handle the pressures and problems, it is an exciting and fulfilling career.

CHAPTER 3

BED BUGS ON THERMOS BOTTLES

Like Chinese puzzle boxes, there are choices within choices that you will address as you prepare for a career in trucking. This chapter will explain some of the most common choices and the potential they hold. The jobs described are, by no means, the only ones available to you. The transportation industry prides itself on creating new ways to define and reward a career in the field. You will also discover, should you choose to drive as a career, that the longer you stay in the business, the more possibilities open up for you. Experience is worth a lot in the transportation industry.

HAULING FREIGHT

First, let's look at the occupational area in terms of equipment and try to define some of the types of hauling jobs available. There are a great many types of trucking. Perhaps the most common is freight hauling. This can entail hauling from coast to coast and across borders to intrastate and local delivery. The proper term for the cargo hauled is general *commodity freight* or, in driver jargon, *dry freight.* In essence, this is freight that does not require any type of specialized handling, such as refrigeration. It may consist of anything from bags of flour to unlabeled tin cans to Sunday supplement pages to the latest European fashions.

Drivers who haul freight face tight delivery deadlines and are usually loaded to the maximum legal weight, since most freight is shipped on a weight/mileage basis. This is also an area where the driver may expect to accept the additional role of freight handler from time to time, since it is often required that a driver load and unload his or her own trailer. The trend in today's trucking business is more and more toward the palletized load, which can be unloaded with forklifts, thus cutting down on labor and time spent at loading docks. Still, conventional freight handling is not an extinct practice, or even a rare one.

When a driver does load or unload, the company the driver hauls for will usually pay extra for this labor. Other companies may consider loading or unloading a part of the job and not directly reimburse the driver. Still other operations will authorize the driver to hire casual labor, or *lumpers,* as they are often called, to load or unload the trailer.

Dry freight operations are for people who like a fast-paced business with little time spent in one location, but who do not want to have to monitor temperatures, check refrigeration fuel and oil levels, and take on other added responsibilities.

A freight hauler's job, however, may include monitoring and counting the number of items or pallets loaded and unloaded from his or her trailer. Merchandise or product count is often very important, and almost all companies require the driver to be present when his or her freight is loaded or unloaded. Usually the driver must also maintain a tally sheet of how much of each item has been entrusted to his or her care. Many companies will hold the driver directly responsible for merchandise lost or damaged and will charge him or her for any shortages that might occur. Often it would be a whole lot more comfortable to be curled up in a nice warm sleeper taking a quick nap, but standing on a cold loading dock counting boxes tends to be one of the jobs that comes with the territory.

REFRIGERATED TRANSPORT

The second most common type of hauling is refrigerated, or perishable, transport. This consists almost exclusively of food items, ranging from meat to produce to frozen goods. They are transported in a refrigerated trailer, giving the driver the added responsibility of monitoring the refrigeration unit, or *reefer,* to ensure the load inside remains at the proper temperature. The cooling unit is usually diesel powered and requires monitoring and periodic maintenance just as the tractor and trailer do. Usually the driver is not responsible for tasks like oil changes or replacing worn belts in the refrigeration unit, but is expected to adjust and maintain the temperature controls, and make sure that oil, fuel, and coolant levels are maintained.

Once again, drivers may be expected to load and unload their own trailers, though this practice is becoming less common, and it is considerably less common with refrigerated loads than with dry freight. It is generally more profitable for a company to *palletize* a load—place the load on wooden skids that can be unloaded, using a forklift or pallet jack, in a matter of minutes.

As stated earlier in this book, you don't have to be a muscle-bound superhero to work in the trucking industry. This is true even of drivers who must load and unload trucks. Most loads, refrigerated or dry, consist of boxes or items that weigh less than fifty pounds apiece. Although unloading 45,000 pounds of freight or produce is no small task, it is far from a physical impossibility for a healthy man or woman. The term "unloading" or "loading" may even be misleading because, most of the time, all the work takes place inside the trailer, transferring boxes or product from a skid to the floor or stacking it from the floor onto a skid, to be hauled away by a forklift operator.

Once again, it is important to note that often the driver is held responsible for the amount of merchandise in the trailer and its condition. It is common to find the driver standing on a loading dock in some cold storage, shifting his or her weight back and forth, trying to keep from freezing to death while keeping tabs on how many boxes of frozen fish sticks are being shoved aboard the trailer. It's not much fun, but it beats paying for a dozen cases of fish sticks that never arrive because they were never loaded, and it is never a wise idea to trust a warehouse worker's word on product count.

FLATBED OPERATIONS

The third major category of hauling is flatbed operations. There are a number of types of flatbeds, ranging from straight flatbeds to drop decks to low boys, designed exclusively for hauling oversized machinery. There is a similarity between freight haulers and refrigerated haulers; at times, they will even haul the same commodities. But neither has much in common with flatbed operations. It is rare, and often impossible, for a flatbed operator to handle his or her own load. However, other physical duties take the place of this chore and may more than make up for the labor that dry or refrigerated freight haulers do. Many flatbed loads require *tarping*—a canvas covering laid over the load and secured with a series of straps and tie-downs—to protect them from the elements. Tarps are heavy and cumbersome, some weighing well over two hundred pounds, and the driver is often seen crawling about the load lugging a tarp, then spending a great deal of time and energy fastening, folding, strapping, cinching, and chaining the load down. The craft of proper tarping is an art form in itself.

In addition, most loads require chaining or strapping to hold them in place on the trailer, and positioning is everything on a flatbed. If the load is out of position, the weight may be off on the axles of the rig, causing it to be overweight or unbalanced (out of trim). If the driver or loader miscalculates, the work may have to be done all over again, which can be extremely frustrating. It doesn't matter if it's 30 degrees below or 110 degrees in the shade; if the loading bills call for tarping, then the load must be tarped. Once again, this is an area where damage to the load is often considered the driver's responsibility.

One major advantage to flatbeds is the loads tend to come off relatively fast. It is not at all unusual for a receiver to have the load off the trailer before the driver has rehung the chains and binders and folded the tarps.

HOUSEHOLD MOVERS

The next most common group of haulers is the household movers. This is among those rare operations that almost always offer training courses. Household movers' duties are different from almost any other operation. They seldom run more than fifty or sixty thousand miles a year. They tend to spend more time inside their trailers than in the cab, and they sit waiting for loads longer than most other truckers. In household operations, the driver is always responsible for loading and unloading his or her own trailer. In fact, it is the loading, unloading, and packing that the household mover depends on to provide a major portion of his or her income. The moving industry is service oriented, but, as in other businesses, there is a price for almost every service rendered.

If you were to watch a mover on a typical day, you might wonder why any sane person would consider the household moving business as an occupation. One answer is money. This is one area where a careful operator can earn an extremely good income. It is also an ideal place for someone who is a "people" person, who likes meeting new people and making new friends. This is one division of the trucking industry that can honestly promise that a driver will work in different parts of the country seldom seen by others in the trucking business. It is also the ideal operation for a husband-and-wife team who are unencumbered by children.

In fact, unofficial statistics indicate that household drivers tend to be young marrieds or newly retired service people. A household mover's biggest expense is generally the fees he or she pays for labor. Once a driver has learned some of the "tricks of the trade," two people can often handle a great many standard loads without hiring that additional (and often expensive) casual labor.

Household movers operate year round, but the busiest time of the year for them is the summer months when kids are out of school and most families plan their moves. In the winter months, the business slows down, but private family moves are replaced by corporate moves, as companies take advantage of reduced winter moving rates.

There is a great deal of physical labor involved and, at times, a household mover will spend a long stretch of time away from home. Six weeks is not at all unusual. This time frame is understandable when you take into account that it may take up to a week to fully load a furniture van to capacity. Modern moving vans and a competent moving professional can fit two, three, four, or more regular households into high-cube trailers, which are often 53 feet long, 13 feet tall, and 108 inches wide.

This is also one area of trucking where mileage is seldom the basis for a paycheck. Normally, a driver will work on a percentage of the *line haul* (the load). Sometimes, a carrier will offer to hire the driver as a *contract driver.* In this case, the operating expenses of the truck—including fuel, labor, and basic maintenance—are paid by the driver. In return, the driver will receive a larger percentage of the load revenue and usually all the peripheral income, such as extra fees movers receive for handling specialty items like pianos or automobiles, or for moving a household from something other than the ground-floor level. These peripheral fees can really add up and often can pay the operating expense of the driver and the rig entirely, leaving the base revenue to send home.

Household movers, due to the nature of their business, tend to be more fraternal than most other drivers or operators. This is partly because of the time they spend together waiting for loads. It is not at all unusual to find a Mayflower, a Wheaton, a United, and an Allied driver sitting at a table together in some truckstop waiting for a call from their individual dispatchers. It is also not unusual to see drivers exchange labor—"I'll help you load yours, if you help me load mine." These exchanges can create tremendous savings for both drivers. Custom usually dictates a steak dinner after the work is over, but a $20 steak is a much better investment than $300 in casual labor fees.

Household movers invest a major amount of time not only learning how to drive, but learning how to load and pack the furniture and goods entrusted to their care. Perhaps because of the extra training requirements—or perhaps because the prospect of what appears to be impossibly hard physical labor scares potential drivers away—household operations tend to be one of the easier fields of trucking to enter.

What is true of refrigerated and dry freight is true tenfold in the moving business. Damage, shortages, and breakage are the mover's nightmare. The paperwork alone is often enough to keep some potential drivers away. It is massive, and it is needed for two main reasons. One is to protect the customer against damage, loss, and claims; the other is to protect the driver against damage, loss, or claims.

Yet, for those who adapt to this unique lifestyle, it is hard to convince them there is a better way to earn a living. The pace goes from hectic to relaxed, and back again. And, because few people actually live on major highways, the householder faces the challenge of taking his or her vehicle into places other trucks would never consider going. Most household drivers tend to consider their group as the elite as far as finesse of driving is concerned. While it may be an arguable point, it's impressive to watch a real professional parallel park a 65-foot tractor-trailer rig on a narrow suburban street.

There are a number of other operations within the trucking industry in addition to the ones already mentioned. We will touch on them lightly, but it should be understood that these areas are somewhat harder to enter, even with truck driving school credentials.

LIQUID BULK OPERATIONS

Liquid bulk operations, commonly referred to as *tankers,* haul commodities ranging from fuel to fish oil to live fish. Special rules and special driving techniques are needed to operate tankers, and a whole new set of DOT requirements apply. While drivers may not physically handle their loads on a tanker, there is plenty to do. Engaging the pump system, measuring tank volume, draining and cleaning the tank and a host of other duties apply. In addition, the driver must observe certain rules that do not necessarily pertain to other types of trucking operations. Tanks tend to be top heavy. Liquid is constantly moving and can cause problems when braking and cornering. Parking or hooking up, or even weather, can be a trial at times. Loads of liquid animal fat, for instance, can solidify during cold weather. Thawing and reliquifying a load can be a frustrating, time-consuming, and nasty business.

HAULING LIVESTOCK

Another area is livestock hauling. Again, this is a specialized field where different rules apply. Livestock—whether sheep, cattle, or hogs—require care and attention. There are rules dictating how often a driver must stop and turn the stock loose for water and/or feed on long trips. A driver must make periodic checks of live cargo to make sure none of the animals has fallen down or injured itself. And finally, just getting to and from a livestock farm—down narrow, rural gravel roads and across wet pastures to reach loading chutes—places this type of driving outside the normal realm of experience. Livestock haulers face the raw adventure of trying to negotiate lanes designed for vehicles one-tenth the weight and a quarter the length of theirs.

However, livestock hauling is one area where an enterprising go-getter might find one of that vanishing breed of owner operators who is willing to train an apprentice. Most livestock hauling companies are small operations with limited budgets and, many times, a family staff. As a driver, you won't make a lot of money, but you will gather valuable experience and, because of the nature of the business, you are almost certain to make close friends.

MULTIPLE TRAILERS

Finally, there are operations that entail hauling multiple trailers, often called *double bottoms.* The problems inherent with a single trailer can be multiplied enormously by adding a second, and sometimes even a third. A driver must think ahead of time before making any move, for if the rig enters an area and the driver suddenly needs to back out, he or she is facing a major headache because double bottoms don't back up well at all. It takes a skilled hand with years of experience to back these monsters with any sort of professionalism. As one driver so aptly put it, "Doubles were created so that aspirin companies would have a steady market to sell to."

THE LOCAL DRIVER

Up to now, we've only discussed the long-haul driver. However, there is another type of driver, more common, in fact, than the long-hauler. The local driver operates under an entirely different set of rules. He or she is paid differently, usually by the hour, and operates differently. Even the equipment is different. If they drive semis at all, local drivers usually use "city" set-ups, which are short wheelbase tractors without sleepers and with smaller horsepower engines. They often pull shorter trailers than their long-haul cousins, to allow them better mobility within the city. A long-hauler may back up to a loading dock two or three times a week. A city driver may double that number before the first morning coffee break. To some, the biggest difference between long-haul and local driving is that the local driver normally gets to sleep at home every night, but the differences are really far greater than that.

While the local driver can generally plan a social and family life by the time clock, there are frustrations here as well. One of the biggest complaints is the boredom of making the same deliveries to the same places day after day, with little or no break in the routine. For some drivers, this is ideal. It means they can plan their days and nights in an orderly fashion. For others, the routine is sheer tedium.

This is also an area where the job market is not quite as active as it is for the long-hauler. Many local driving jobs are unionized, and a system of seniority has been long established, which can make it difficult for the new driver to break into the field.

Another somewhat negative aspect is that if a driver takes a job with a smaller company, the rate of pay may not be all that great. However, pay may not be a deciding factor in some cases.

For the person who wants to get into long hauling, local driving offers one advantage we talked about earlier: experience. While your image of trucking may not include making three mile runs with 16 stops to load or unload along the way, it is an excellent training ground for a new driver to learn some of the more difficult aspects of the occupation. Backing a truck squarely up to a loading dock, operating in heavy traffic, and negotiating narrow streets and their accompanying hazards are some of the many difficulties a local driver learns to overcome as he or she gains experience. For many road drivers, these skills are the toughest part of the job, which can make local hauling an extremely valuable experience for someone who wants to eventually work the long-haul side of the business.

Obviously, not all local delivery is done with a tractor-trailer rig. Straight trucks, sometimes called *bobtails,* commonly haul freight within local areas. While these vehicles do not pose all the problems a driver would face with semis, they do challenge a driver, and they carry their own set of headaches with them. One of the biggest is the fact that straight trucks are expected to go where tractor-trailers can't, and in some of our older cities, narrow streets, low underpasses, and other hazards are far more common for the local hauler than they are for the over-the-road trucker. Creeping down an alley with your side mirrors scraping bricks on both sides can be every bit as challenging as maneuvering a semi over some rain-slicked mountain pass.

Almost all forms of local hauling require loading and unloading. It goes with the job. Here, too, keeping accurate inventory of what you pick up and drop off *before* you sign for it is of paramount importance. It is uncommon for local carriers to charge shortages against paychecks, since there are more local drivers available. However, shortages can mean that the company will simply fire you and replace you with someone who will pay attention to "load and count."

THE CONSTRUCTION DRIVER

Before we leave this chapter, we'll touch briefly on one other type of driver: the construction driver. Generally speaking, these are drivers who haul items to and from job sites. The load may be gravel, cement, lumber, or backhoes, but it is all somewhat specialized. This is one of the few areas where someone who is under 21 may find employment, though this, too, is becoming rarer by the day. Quite often, construction driving takes place as part of other duties pertinent to a job site. You might be laying blacktop for a driveway when the job foreman asks for another load of gravel and sends you off to pick it up. Or it may be a major operation where you simply load, drive a few miles, unload, return, empty, and repeat the cycle all over again. The commercial operators license is still necessary, but if the driving all takes place within the state, other DOT requirements, such as log books, may not apply.

Construction driving is not the same as road operations and should not be mistaken for it, but it does provide experience behind the wheel on a vehicle that has size, weight, and the general qualities of a road rig. It is enough to provide that general base experience that all employers want to see a resume or an application. As a rule, it also pays quite well, but tends to be somewhat seasonal.

This chapter has barely scratched the surface of driver requirements and some of the highpoints of what is available to a driver within the trucking industry. For many drivers, perhaps the majority, the starting point will not necessarily be the final career choice. Driving is, for many, the first step toward a career in one of the administrative positions within the business. For instance, a driver trainer cannot become an instructor without first getting actual road experience. It is difficult, if not impossible, for a safety person to attain that position without first experiencing and learning first-hand the actual applications of the federal and state requirements through driving experience. In short, a driver can gain experience and step into many of the transportation positions that exist within a trucking company, or in the transportation field in general.

Driving is not a permanent sight-seeing excursion. It is not a way to get rich quick. It is not a career for the lazy, nor is it a job for someone who places his or her social life above all other things. It is not a career for someone whose spouse cannot deal with the absence of his or her partner for extended periods. And it is not a career for anyone who lacks basic organizational skills. After all, you may be out on the road when the rent comes due, and it's up to you to think ahead and plan for these things. If you can't or won't, perhaps you should consider another line of work.

The next chapter will deal with the financial realities of a career in driving. Not everyone is cut out to be a driver, but if you are, it opens the door to a vast area of career opportunities.

CHAPTER 4

BIG BUCKS: FACT OR MYTH?

If you decide to pursue a career in driving, a number of decisions will face you that have never been part of your occupational life before. Obviously, one of the first decisions will involve training. We've already discussed the things to watch for and to avoid, but now it is time to see what follows the training period and what to expect.

Since no one works for free, the obvious first consideration is money. Here the industry, at least to the novice, looks imminently confusing, so let's take a good, hard look at the various payment structures within the business.

MILEAGE AND BONUSES

As mentioned earlier, the simplest and most common payment for driving is based on mileage. Some companies offer a simple, straight-forward, base-rate figure for miles driven, based on the *Household Mover's Mileage Guide* or "PC Miler." Today, the average starting wage runs somewhere in the area of 27 to 32 cents per mile. Sometimes it's less, sometimes considerably more. But the "simple" mileage payment seems to be rapidly vanishing from the scene.

Today, driver's wage plans tend to look more like automobile rebate systems than income rates. For instance, it is very common for a carrier to offer a 25 cents-per-mile base rate, than add a number of incentive incomes to reward consistent, profitable, and safe work. For example, the driver may receive an additional cent per mile for attaining a miles-per-gallon efficiency. This is done by maintaining a constant, economical driving speed and by not needlessly allowing the engine to idle when the truck is parked. If the driver has the option of buying fuel when and where he or she wants, an additional cent may be added for keeping the cost of fuel below a certain price per gallon. Some companies, such as J.B. Hunt, have a computerized log built into the truck. When the vehicle reaches a terminal, the "computer log" is read. The company may pay bonuses, or perhaps penalize a driver, for maintaining or failing to maintain certain operating speeds and RPMs. Some drivers see this as the "Big Brother is watching" approach to income, and others view it as challenging their skills. It is a matter of viewpoint. No matter how you may view it, however, this is the trend of the future and a growing number of carriers are moving in this direction.

All companies are vitally concerned with safety. As insurance costs continue to soar, safety bonuses are becoming increasingly important, which, from a driver's point of view, translates into more money. These bonuses are usually based on mileage accumulated over a long period of time, usually quarterly or semiannually. Most safety bonuses are paid as one or two cents per mile for every safety period the driver operates without an accident, without a traffic citation from any law enforcement agency.

Some companies will also reward a driver for maintaining his or her log book without any appreciable errors. These bonuses can be quite large, and not all are paid in the form of cash. There is a growing tendency to offer drivers paid vacations and other "perks" that until a few years ago were unheard of in the industry except for trucking executives.

Another bonus may come from load-handling expertise. Since damaged goods do not sell, the cargo the driver hauls also enters into the payment structure, and a claims bonus may be paid, again on a quarterly or even an annual basis. If there is no loss or breakage or damage, the company will pay the driver a certain amount per mile.

Paperwork is the bane of all drivers. It tends to be the last thing any driver wants to handle, yet it is precisely what pays the bills for most companies. In addition, because federal and state governments take such an interest in the trucking business, it is bound to be loaded down with mounds of paperwork. Therefore, a number of companies offer a bonus for paperwork turned in on time and filled in properly. This includes not only the bills of lading, but the other paperwork involved with the truck, such as log books and maintenance records. Other companies may approach the situation from the other direction, by penalizing the driver for turning in paperwork late. It's all a matter of approach and philosophy.

As mentioned in the first chapter, driving can keep you out and away from home for long periods of time. To compensate for this, many companies offer incentives for the number of miles legally logged during any month. The figure usually starts at 8,000 to 10,000 miles, and payment, called a *mileage bonus,* is based on miles run over that figure. If a driver can maintain an average of 10,000 miles per month, it is possible to accumulate a very respectable bonus figure, because miles translate to dollars to a trucking company.

As mentioned earlier, not all bonuses involve money. Some companies compensate their drivers by paying in "bonus days." If a driver operates, for instance, for two weeks out on the road away from home, the company may offer three or four uninterrupted days off when the driver arrives back at home terminal. Usually, these are not paid days, but merely compensation in the form of time off to allow the driver to catch up on home life and unwind from the hectic pace of highway living.

TEAM DRIVERS

Not all drivers drive solo. Some form one-half of a team operation. Almost all team drivers receive bonus compensation of one sort or another. Of all the methods of trucking, team driving is one of the most grueling.

A truck that operates with two drivers has special problems not encountered in solo operations. Generally, the company will attempt to load, unload, and reload the team operated rig as quickly as possible to maintain maximum efficiency. For teams, mileage is everything. It is almost impossible to run out of legal hours driving team, so the name of the game when driving team is to log as many miles as possible with as few delays as possible. Most team operations run longer trips than solo driver operations—generally over a thousand miles from point to point, or more.

Team operators are paid in much the same way as solo drivers, but with two important differences. The first is that in some team operations, there is a classification of the two drivers, one being *first seat* and the other being *second seat.* First-seat drivers tend to be the more experienced and may be referred to as *lead drivers.* Because of their experience, they are paid more than the second-seat driver. Usually, there is a mileage rate split offered a team operation. For instance, if the rate is 35 cents per mile, the first driver may get 19 cents while the second seat may get 16 cents.

At first glance, it might seem as though team operations would log double the mileage of a solo operator. This is not the case. The reason is fairly simple, though not immediately evident. Even though a team may cover many more miles in a 24-hour period than a solo driver—a team can load in Los Angeles on Monday morning and be in New York for Wednesday delivery—they have to allow time for meals, for switching drivers, for fueling, and, most of all, for loading and unloading. Each time a load is placed on or taken off the trailer, time is eaten up that could have been spent on the road. Service work on the truck, time spent waiting for loads to become available, weather, and other factors all affect the number of miles that can be run. The average team freight operation runs somewhere between 150,000 and 170,000 miles per year, compared to about 100,000 to 115,000 for a solo operator. With larger companies, trailers are maintained all over the country and instead of loading or unloading, a team may just "drop and hook." That is, they will drop their loaded trailer and pick up another preloaded trailer while a local driver makes the actual delivery. You should pay close attention to what a company offers when comparing team with solo operations.

There are advantages and disadvantages to operating as a team. One major advantage occurs when a husband and wife team up to run together. Obviously, the money earned stays in the family. If we use the figure of 170,000 paid miles per year at a combined total of 36 cents per mile, a husband-and-wife team can gross a very respectable $61,300 per year before expenses and taxes. In addition, husband-and-wife team operations are actively solicited by many companies on the theory that these teams are less likely to become antagonized by each other, and they will pay closer attention to the truck and to their road expenses. Over the years, this theory has justified itself many times over.

Another factor to consider is that most team operations are offered a higher per-mile base wage than solo drivers, as a way of compensating for the fewer individual average miles. Most companies compensate their drivers so that even second-seat drivers can at least earn a living from their efforts and justify being out on the road.

The biggest potential disadvantage for team operators lies in the area of personality. It is not always easy to share the confined quarters of a truck cab with a person mile after mile, week after week. The other driver may not drive the same way you do, may not like to stop where you want to stop, or may not have the same personal habits—such as smoking, or even something as simple as driving with the window up or down. In some companies, you are given no choice whatsoever in partners. It's simply the luck of the draw. In others, you may be able to pick and choose partners. Running team can be a very profitable way of driving a truck, but it can also wear on your nerves. It is a fast-paced, deadline-to-deadline existence, and it is not for everyone.

PERCENTAGE COMPENSATION

Another popular method of payment is the percentage. Percentage is, very simply, a portion of the earnings—called *line haul* in transportation lingo—earned from each load the truck carries. In other words, your income is based on how well the truck is compensated. Usually, this compensation begins somewhere around 20 or 25 percent, and up. It can entail all kinds of variations. The most common place for a driver to find percentage compensation is with the furniture moving industry.

This is probably a good place to insert a word or two about companies and their motives for paying the way they do. You must understand that all trucking companies are in business to make money. As already touched upon, there is very high driver turnover within the industry, and companies are unwilling to make a major investment in someone who may or may not stick around for long. Therefore, they design their payment systems accordingly. If the company pays by mileage, they, as a company, are generally paid in percentages, and mileage is the less expensive way of paying a driver. If the company specializes in discounting the freight it handles, it usually will pay in percentage because it is the smaller portion of investment in a driver for them. This may sound cold or harsh, but it is, nonetheless, the reality of the business. In short, as an untried commodity, the trucking company will pay you as little as possible until you have proved your worth. In reality, this is precisely what any other business does with a new employee. They just aren't quite so brutally blunt about it.

Percentage payment generally doesn't include bonuses, or may include specific bonuses that are paid only periodically. A percentage payment involves one other major disadvantage. If you have to travel empty from one point to another, you are, in effect, doing it for free. Even in some mileage payment plans, your income may be based on *loaded miles.* Miles traveled without a load are called *deadhead miles,* and no company earns anything by hauling around an empty trailer.

CONTRACT DRIVERS

Another method of payment can take the form of either a percentage, which is most common, or a figure per mile. The job title is contract driver, and it can be set up in a number of ways. Most contract drivers are not considered employees of the company. Therefore, they are paid as contractors, and no taxes are withheld from their paychecks. They may receive considerably more money per load or trip than a driver/employee, but they also face additional expenses. This type of payment is most common in the household moving industry, but recently has drifted into a number of other trucking operations.

It should be understood up front that a contract driver assumes a number of responsibilities. Personal insurance coverage, for example, is usually the driver's own responsibility. It is extremely difficult for a trucker to claim workman's compensation while functioning as a contract driver. And normally, if a contract driver hits a period of doldrums, where loads are scarce, he or she must be able to make cash stretch, because chances of getting any help in the meantime from the carrier are slim.

Contract driving works like this: A driver is offered 35 to 50 percent of the line haul. From that, the driver must pay for fuel, hired labor, road expenses, tolls, and most of the everyday expenses incurred during the operation of the truck, including little things like replacing dome lights or changing oil. Usually, the company will pay the expense of owner-related items like fuel permits; licensing; major repair items, such as engine overhauls; and tires.

Since this method is most common in the household moving industry, let's look at the way this plan works using a moving company contract driver as an example. Household rates are based on a combination of factors, including a complicated weight/mileage ratio. Movers can generally haul more than one household in their vans, and the smaller the load, the higher the rate per pound/mile. It is common to find a loaded trailer netting a gross of $7,000 revenue or more. If the contract driver is receiving 35 percent, his or her share is $2,450. From this, the driver must pay for labor—call it $350 spent loading and another $250 unloading—fuel of perhaps

$400, and maybe a week of road expense at $25 per day, for a total of $1,175. Add in the fact that the driver probably spent a week putting the load together for an additional $175. These total expenses of $1,350, leave the driver with a two-week earning of $1,100 before taxes. In addition to this profit, the driver receives from 80 to 100 percent of the income generated by items such as stairway or elevator charges, packing or unpacking, and other fees charged to moving customers. In the example above, these extra fees might equal $200. So the driver had what amounts to about a weeks' living expense in the household business. During the summer's heaviest running, this would be considered a rather poor earning period, but overall, it's probably close to the yearly average.

OWNER/OPERATORS

There is another earning method, or more accurately, another way of entering the trucking business. That is as an owner/operator. This might sound nearly impossible, since a new truck can easily cost $100,000 or more, but there are some companies that offer to set a driver up in business. Mayflower, North American Van Lines, Wheaton, Schneider, and many more have drivers' purchase plans that allow people with a little money and a lot of ambition to go into business for themselves.

Some include training in the purchase package, and the down payments required are generally quite low in comparison with what a rig would cost through normal channels.

Normally, you are only buying the tractor. You will agree to haul company trailers at a specific rate or percentage. The company generally maintains their portion of the equipment at their expense, except, perhaps, for tires and load insurance. Meanwhile, you are held responsible for the expense and upkeep of your tractor and possibly any specialty equipment you may need, such as load locks to hold loads in place and padlocks for securing the trailer doors.

There are, of course, catches to these programs. First, and most important, is the fact that, though you may be making the payments on that truck, you are still essentially under the direct control of the company who provided the program. This means, among other things, that should you decide to leave the company, you will either have to pay the truck off in full—that is, cough up as much as $60,000 to $80,000 or more on the spot—or turn it back in to the company, usually with nothing back no matter how much or little is owed against the rig.

Most banks are less than enthusiastic about refinancing a tractor, and few of us have the cash on hand to simply pay off a loan of this size. In addition, you will not be able to haul for any other company as long as the truck is financed by your carrier because the truck is leased directly to the carrier. In essence, you have married that carrier, so make sure before you invest that this is an operation you will want to work with for the next three to five years. In becoming an owner/operator, you are assuming a financial responsibility that can lead to much better things, but it can also blow up in your face, leaving you disillusioned and, worse, with your credit in shreds for years.

Even when things go well, owning a truck carries with it its own special problems and responsibilities. One of the more important considerations is maintenance and repair. It is said with some accuracy that nothing on a truck is cheap. Starters cost $800. Tires run in excess of $250 apiece. Just washing a rig costs around $50 or $60, and changing the oil is more than a $100 investment if it's done in a shop. If you enter into a lease/purchase program, these repair and maintenance costs become your responsibility. Should you "blow" an engine, figure it will cost more than $7,000 to rebuild, *if* it can be done with the engine block still mounted within the chassis. If the engine has to be pulled from the frame, add $2,000 to $3,000 or even more to the cost.

Add to the cost of repairs the fact that while the rig is in the shop—which can run into weeks—you are not on the road, and therefore you are not earning anything. There is no insurance to cover this sort of thing, and even though the tractor may be under warranty, the warranty doesn't cover your personal, out-of-pocket expenses while the rig is being repaired. There are serious risks to consider here.

Even if the rig runs just fine, the everyday costs are considerable. Some companies pay for permits and special licensing. Others don't. A trucker licensed to haul through all 48 continental states will spend in excess of $7,500 for licensing, and an additional $5,000 to $7,000 or more for insurance. A round trip for a loaded tractor/trailer from Washington, D.C., to Columbus, Ohio, via toll roads will cost nearly $200 in tolls. As you can see, there is truth to the statement that absolutely nothing is cheap when you're maintaining or operating a tractor-trailer rig.

But it is easier to see by example the actual operating costs. Consider these figures from a typical freight operation running 115,000 miles per year in 48 states.

MONTHLY EXPENSES
OF OWNER/OPERATOR

Item	Cost
Base Plate and Permits	$200
Payment on Rig	$2,500
Insurance	$500
Fuel	$1,900
Maintenance	$700
Tolls and Personal Expenses	$950
MONTHLY TOTAL	$6,750
YEARLY TOTAL	$81,000

Notice the table of expenses doesn't count things like motels, labor, damage claims, and other typical expenses. Most importantly, it doesn't include the money everyone needs to pay their household expenses away from the truck. If a driver needs an additional $24,000 in wages to meet personal needs, he or she must gross about $105,000 a year. Even in this "ideal" set-up, the truck must average no less than 91 cents per actual mile, or about $1.07 cents per book mile.

Another risk to consider is the market itself. If your rig is empty and you're sitting still in some truckstop, you are not making any money, but the truck's payment will be due at the end of the month, just like always. The trucking industry is subject to ups and downs just like the stock market. You may be busy one week and spend the next desperately trying to find something—anything—to put in your trailer to earn a buck.

There are also serious considerations and benefits on the other side of the coin. First is pride of ownership. Even though you are somewhat under company control, the fact is that the truck is yours, and some day you plan to hold free and clear title to it. And once the truck is paid for, it's a rolling savings account. If you can manage to maintain a truck until it is free and clear of encumbrance, the payments you have been making—which can easily amount to as much as $3,000 per month—can be put away in a savings account. There is still a good market for used trucks, and a five-year-old truck today is worth anywhere from $22,000 to $35,000, depending on brand, how it's equipped, and what kind of mechanical condition it is in. So the truck's resale value also can be counted as part of your overall earnings as an owner/operator.

It takes confidence, careful planning, and just a little luck to make everything come together the way you want. If you are hooked up with a good company, they'll help you all they can, within reason. It's to their advantage to have you succeed and stay with them for the long term.

The bottom line is still money. The owner/operators have the best chance of earning the best living of all drivers, for they can control their own destiny to some degree. Under ideal conditions, before-tax earnings may approach $40,000 or even $60,000 after all expenses are accounted for, *if* the operator is both cautious and willing to stay out and run when others are looking for that weekly load home. It is a matter of placing business first, above almost everything, including social obligations, vacations, even birthdays and anniversaries and holidays. As an owner/operator, you are a self-employed businessperson. Your truck payments and the interest on the load for your rig won't take a day off, so plan your leisure time very carefully. You'll have three to five years to pay off an amount most folks would consider the size of a fairly hefty house mortgage. That gives you some perspective on the amount of obligation you've accepted when you become an owner/operator.

An owner/operator, even when he or she is home, is still responsible for the rig. It is part of the obligation being an owner entails. This means that maintenance you can do yourself needs to be done when you are home, and you may find your family doesn't fully comprehend the necessity of this. Family and friends may accuse you of spending more time with the truck than you do with them. Like most successful business owners, owner/operators spend most of their time looking after their business. The problem is that it's sometimes hard to remember the truck is a business, and not simply a vehicle.

LET THE DRIVER BEWARE

So far, this chapter has highlighted some of the options you will have once you've made the commitment to drive, and some of the risks, rewards, problems, and pitfalls you'll face. Under no circumstances is this the definitive catch-all for the industry and the offers and payment plans available. Nor does it explain every scam and come-on you might run into. For instance, nothing was said about driver bonus plans that are literally unattainable. Not every company is scrupulous in their dealings with drivers. Common bonus scams include offering bonuses for more miles than can be legally run during the period. A driver is bound by federal decree to not exceed so many hours of operation within a 24-hour period, or a week, or an eight-day stretch of driving.

Another bad program, though not precisely a scam, is a bonus plan that requires the driver to meet every criteria—from on-time delivery to matching the minimum mileage to maintaining the proper fuel/cost ratio—before *any* bonus at all is earned. This is an all-or-nothing program, and often it is all but impossible to meet all the requirements within the time-frame required.

What it boils down to is that the driver needs to be wary and ask questions, not just of the employment personnel but of other drivers who have been with the company for a while, and perhaps drivers who have left the company, if they can be found. Keep in mind when talking to a driver who has quit or been fired from a trucking operation that this driver is most likely unhappy with the operation and may or may not represent the facts fairly. While scams can be found within the industry, it is far more common to find ex-drivers with a simple case of "sour grapes." It is up to you to do your homework. Check the company out as thoroughly as they are checking your background.

There are risks in any venture, and trucking is no exception. If you are offered a driving job with a bonus factor as part of the payment package, study it. Then decide, based on what you know, what others have said, and, perhaps most importantly, how you feel. If things have been described in rosy, glowing terms, and the job simply sounds too good to be true, it probably is. Trucking is hard, difficult work, and there are many risk factors to take into consideration. It can also be fulfilling, profitable, and, at times, even fun. Mental attitude has a lot to do with how you perform as a trucker.

CHAPTER 5

TRUCKING'S MOST HATED?

Not every job within the trucking industry involves driving. In fact, though drivers are the backbone of the industry, and certainly the most visible people in the business, they operate only with a massive support base. A key figure within that base is the *dispatcher.*

It's not enough to have a driver for each truck in the fleet. Somewhere along the line, someone has to tell the driver of that truck where to go to pick up a load, and where to drop it off. A dispatcher's job appears simple when you only look at the end results. After all, how difficult can it be to tell a driver where his or her next load is?

A dispatcher might say, "Drive to Buffalo, pick up 45,000 pounds of widgets from XYZ Company, and deliver them to Chicago to ABC Incorporated by 7 A.M. Monday." What many don't realize is the work entailed to reach the point where the load is actually dispatched. Sometimes, especially with the smaller operations, the dispatcher's job may overlap into other areas, such as planning, rating, and even marketing. However, for our purposes, we will deal only with the dispatcher's basic functions and enter the world of planning, sales, and logistics in a later chapter.

JOB REQUIREMENTS

A dispatcher's function includes seeing to it that the trucks under his or her control are loaded in a fair, timely, and economical fashion, then sent or dispatched to another location where they will be unloaded and reloaded, again in the most profitable fashion. A dispatcher constantly operates under pressure, so if you are easily angered or stressed, this is certainly not a field for you to consider.

In addition, a dispatcher is arguably the most "disliked" person in the trucking family tree. After all, this is the only person a driver deals with directly on a regular basis and also the person the shipper or receiver contacts when there is a problem with a load. Dispatching a driver to New York, when you know that driver despises running "dirtyside," or attempting to explain to a shipper why a load hasn't arrived and the driver has yet to call in to let you know where, precisely, the load is, can lead to angry words and a great deal of stress. If your personality doesn't deal well with these factors, dispatching is hardly the place for you.

Although geography is no longer a required course in many schools, a dispatcher needs to know a great deal about the topic to function well at his or her profession. For instance, if the dispatcher has an empty truck and driver in Houston, he or she would be well advised not to send that rig to El Paso to pick up a load, even though both cities are located in Texas. Why? El Paso, Texas, is over eight hundred miles from Houston. At five miles to the gallon and an average speed of 50 miles per hour, it will take the driver nearly 16 hours and a whopping 160 gallons of fuel to make the drive, running empty—in other words, for free—every foot of the way. This is extremely unprofitable, and efficient dispatchers are painfully aware that their continued employment and income are directly linked to the profitability of the trucks in their charge.

The dispatcher also needs to possess decent business math skills in addition to geography and the obvious communication skills. Numbers play an important role in the everyday functions of the job, from figuring weight to calculating distances and time of travel. Also, as more and more businesses turn to computerized filing systems and workstations, most dispatchers in major companies and an ever-increasing number of small companies work from a computer console where at least minimal keyboarding skills are necessary. Most high schools and all community colleges offer instruction in this type of office skill, and if you don't possess it, it's a good idea to pick it up.

ROUTING TRUCKS

The easiest way to explain a dispatcher's function is to follow a series of loads once they reach the dispatch area. For the most part, dispatchers are assigned in one of two ways. Either they handle specific trucks and drivers, or they are responsible for specific geographic areas, usually called zones or regions. Depending again on the size and operating area of the company, this may mean one or two states, or even a handful of cities, or it may entail a massive portion of the country.

For this example, let's assume that the dispatcher is responsible for a specific group of drivers. Driver A calls dispatch at 7 A.M. from Detroit and reports that the truck will be empty within an hour. The dispatcher takes the information and compares it with the other trucks and drivers in the Detroit area under his or her responsibility. The dispatcher sees that Driver B unloaded in Detroit yesterday afternoon and therefore is first in line for a load. Generally, the dispatcher will also have other information about the truck and driver, such as how long the driver has been out on the road since last stopping at home, where the driver lives, how many hours of service remain according to the driver's log books, and when the truck or trailer was last in a terminal or maintenance shop for servicing. All these factors and more have a bearing on the decisions the dispatcher will eventually face when dispatching Driver A's next load.

Next, the dispatcher consults the load board. Before the age of computers, this was a large slotted board where planners would place three-by-five cards detailing available loads. These days, load boards are usually not boards at all, but computer screens, and the cards show up as geographically assigned loads available. These loads are arranged according to pick-up dates, delivery points, and other factors. But the term still remains, and electronic or not, they are still called boards.

In our example, there is only one load available, and it's in Ann Arbor. The dispatcher has a quick decision to make; in this case, it's an easy one. Since Driver A is not yet empty, the Ann Arbor load should go to Driver B. The dispatcher tells Driver A to finish unloading, then call back in an hour.

Meanwhile, Driver B calls in, and the dispatcher describes the load in Ann Arbor. Sometimes it is the driver's responsibility to contact a shipper, but more often than not, it is the dispatcher's job. Driver B agrees to take the load. Now the dispatcher has to take into account the number of miles from Detroit to Ann Arbor and also the fact that it is the busiest time of the morning, and traffic will slow Driver B's arrival time. The dispatcher calls the shipper and gives them an estimate of what time to expect the driver, then returns to the load board and checks the number of drivers remaining who are empty from the day before, and perhaps again checks for a Detroit area load for Driver A. There is still nothing showing on the board, but the dispatcher logs Driver A's truck in as empty in case someone in marketing or planning or perhaps in another dispatch area comes up with a load in the region not covered by another driver.

CUSTOMER SERVICE

Now a customer in Des Moines calls and wants to know where his truckload of widgets are; they were due at his warehouse an hour ago.

In all likelihood, in this day and age where electronic marvels are commonplace, the dispatcher will have some sort of a "voice mail" system to help him or her communicate with drivers even after normal operating hours. Generally, voice mail, or messages left by whatever night crew the company employs to monitor the phone, is the first thing a dispatcher checks when on arriving at work. Voice mail messages can prepare the dispatcher to answer questions such as the one posed by the Des Moines customer. However, if voice mail isn't installed in this office, or the driver has failed to call in, the dispatcher may face the difficult situation of trying to placate an irate customer while fervently hoping the driver will eventually show up or call in and at least let dispatch know the load's status.

In this case, the dispatcher checks the files for the load and discovers that Driver Z was to have delivered that load this morning, but has not shown up yet. The dispatcher checks for messages and discovers Driver Z called in at about 4 A.M. and reported a tire blowout and that no tire dealers would be open for another four hours. The driver is in Omaha, which tells the dispatcher it will take at least an hour to change the tire, four hours to drive to Des Moines, and probably an extra hour to deal with city traffic. The dispatcher calls the customer, explains the situation, and gives the customer a new ETA—estimated time of arrival.

The customer is furious. He has hired extra help specifically to unload that trailer when it arrived. Now he's going to be forced to pay almost a day's wages to his extra help. The dispatcher tries to calm the customer, then contacts customer service and claims to pass along the information and notify them of a possible claim pending on load number 123 from LMN Company. The dispatcher offers customer service a brief explanation of the circumstances surrounding the incident.

DISPATCH DECISIONS

Meanwhile, Driver A calls in again, and Driver C is on the other line, reporting empty in Denver. There is still nothing available on the Detroit load board covering Driver A's region, and dispatch tells Driver A to call in another hour. The Denver area has a partial shipment available, so the dispatcher checks the load board to see if there is another partial shipment in the Denver area destined for the same region and if it can be hauled with the first partial. These partial loads are called *LTLs,* or *less-than-a-load shipments,* and are very profitable for companies since they are shipped at a higher rate per mile or pound—a penalty for the hassle of working with partial shipments. The dispatcher discovers there is a second load available in Cheyenne, Wyoming, about a three-hour drive from Denver.

The dispatcher glances at the clock. Dispatch is on Central time, and it's 7:30 A.M., which means it's 6:30 in Denver. It will take three hours to load the Denver portion of the load into Driver C's trailer and another three hours to reach Cheyenne, making Driver C's ETA 12:30 P.M. at Cheyenne. The dispatcher tells Driver C where the loads are, where they are going, and other information necessary for the driver to operate efficiently. The dispatcher then tells "C" to call back when the first shipment is loaded. Then the dispatcher calls the shipper in Cheyenne and gives them the information on the truck in Denver, including an ETA from Denver to Cheyenne. The shipper agrees that the ETA is acceptable, and the dispatcher marks the load off as assigned to Driver C on the load board.

Then Driver W calls in empty. The driver is in El Paso and wants to go home to St. Paul. The dispatcher knows it's difficult to get direct loads from West Texas to Minnesota this time of year, so the dispatcher asks if it would be okay to route the driver out of El Paso with a load to Louisiana, then, from there, to St. Paul. Or would Driver W rather wait in El Paso and see if a load going north becomes available? The driver is smart and takes the load available immediately, but has the dispatcher reserve a northbound load, from Louisiana if possible. The dispatcher checks the load board for future bookings, finds a shipment scheduled for pick up in three days, and tentatively marks the load for Driver W.

Here the dispatcher has to use some judgment. Is Driver W dependable? Does the driver make deliveries on time? Is Driver W responsible and easily located? At the same time, there are other dispatchers with their own drivers to look after. The dispatcher cannot afford to mark this load down for Driver W if another driver under another dispatcher will be there sooner and therefore ahead of the line on the load board. Again, thanks to the computer, the dispatcher can flag the load, notifying fellow dispatchers that, unless they have an overriding situation, that load will be reserved for Driver W.

In this case, when the dispatcher marks the load in Louisiana as "flagged," another dispatcher notices the flag. This other dispatcher has a driver in the same situation, but who will deliver in New Orleans the next morning. Depending on company policy, the load will either be held on a first come, first serve basis, or reserved according to either the seniority or the reliability of the driver.

One of the biggest challenges faced by any dispatcher is maintaining a good working relationship with his or her drivers and other co-workers. A dispatcher must remain constantly aware of the many problems faced by drivers, shippers, receivers, and also, above all, keep in mind the bottom line—the profitability of each decision and its benefit to the company as a whole. Will shipping a load with this driver on this truck made money for the company? It is a fine line the dispatcher has to walk, and often he or she must have thick skin because it's not possible to please everybody every time. In short, dispatchers tend to get yelled at a lot.

EARNINGS

A dispatcher's life is a fast-paced affair of ringing phones and constantly changing load boards. Pay for a "green" dispatcher is not overwhelmingly good; it depends a great deal on the size of the company and the duties and responsibilities of the dispatch office. Base pay is usually no less than $15,000 a year and often somewhat more. Raises come fairly quickly once a new dispatcher has gained some necessary working experience. Most people trying to enter the field find it easiest to find their first job with a smaller company, since major carriers prefer to work with seasoned professionals. However, once a dispatcher has some experience, those skills are valuable, and pay climbs rapidly. Wages of $30,000, and more, are not unusual.

Though the practice seems to be fading in favor of a salaried or hourly wage, some dispatchers do continue to work on a commission basis, not unlike salespeople. Their income is based on the line haul of the loads they dispatch. Generally speaking, dispatchers who receive a commission also book loads for their drivers outside of the company. This practice is known as *trip leasing* and quite simply means that dispatchers call other companies looking for a load in the area where they have a driver.

These loads become available when a company overbooks what they can actually haul. Usually they will list these loads as available to other companies at a percentage of what they've sold the load for. Trip leases are generally not popular with drivers who work on a percentage, nor are they very popular with the carrier, both of whom are, in effect, sharing a portion of the proceeds with the original booker.

Like it or not, trip leasing is a very common practice. It's so common, in fact, that there are people called brokers who do nothing but book loads, then sell them to carriers and independent operators on a trip-lease basis at a discounted rate. Brokers earn their living from the difference between what they booked the load for, and what they pay the carrier to haul it. Dispatching a truck and driver on a trip-leased load is the next to last choice favored by companies, drivers, or dispatchers. The last choice is to *deadhead*—that is, to run the truck empty—to a distant location to pick up a load in a more favorable market.

CAREER OPTIONS

If your goal is to eventually enter an administrative position within a trucking company, dispatch is an excellent place to begin. A dispatcher is almost guaranteed to pick up the requirements, skills, and information needed to enter other fields within the industry—from marketing to rating. Dispatching allows a person to see almost every aspect of the trucking business in action, but it's not an occupation for those with hot tempers or those who are easily flustered. Nor is dispatching necessarily a job for those who want to walk out the office door at the end of eight hours.

A dispatcher carries a lot of responsibility on his or her shoulders. In order to meet deadlines and get drivers loaded, or even because of time zone differences, a dispatcher may have to work over and above the allotted eight-hour day. In some major companies, with customer bases across the country, it is not unusual to find a dispatcher working from 7 A.M. to well after 8 P.M. It is also very common to maintain a weekend dispatch in many companies. Some even have a 24-hour, around-the-clock dispatching staff on duty as more and more international markets open up. Other companies with smaller staffs may rotate the duties. Some dispatchers simply add an extra day to their work load, perhaps working one weekend day every third week, or once a month, or some similar arrangement. There are few clock-watchers among top-notch dispatchers.

Of course, a dispatcher can be male or female, and here, unlike driving, age is not an immediate barrier, though most companies prefer people with some formal schooling. In some areas, college students can work as dispatchers, or in other departments of the business, as part of their college credits. For those majoring in transportation or similar fields of logistics, dispatching is an excellent training ground, and some of the major transportation companies even offer internships for full-time students.

Trucking dispatchers can also apply their skills to careers outside of the trucking industry. Dispatching for a trucking operation is very similar to dispatching or working logistics for any type of transportation business—from aviation to maritime to metropolitan transportation systems. In short, depending on your career goals, dispatching is an excellent place to begin your transportation career.

ADVANCES IN TECHNOLOGY

A word here concerning electronics and computers that applies not only to dispatch positions, but is rapidly becoming standard throughout every career choice within the transportation industry. As the world of technology improves, and electronic wizardry becomes more commonplace and affordable, trucking companies are relying more and more on the marvels of the age to ensure maximum efficiency within every aspect of the industry. In addition, shippers are demanding more accountability from trucking companies entrusted with their products. Most meat packing companies, such as IBP and Farmland and others, now require trucking companies to outfit their equipment with satellite positioning systems so that a dispatcher can tell at a glance exactly where a specific load of meat is located.

As this industry continues to expand, more and more trucks are equipped with computers, satellite locating systems, and on-board communication links. The days of waiting for a driver to call in, or for a dispatcher to call a driver back are rapidly being replaced with electronic dispatch where a driver actually receives his or her bills of lading and trip sheets via fax and computer while sitting in the truck. Dispatchers can punch a couple keys and immediately locate the load—within a handful of feet anywhere in the United States or Canada, read the temperature of a refrigerated load, ascertain the oil level of a truck engine, or determine the speed of the truck as it moves down a highway.

This is not a fad, but the wave of the future. In short, new careers are opening up daily within the electronic and technical communication fields. In addition, for the person who intends to make a career of the trucking business, whether driver, dispatcher, salesperson or even maintenance, computer savvy is becoming essential just to survive, let alone compete. Even payroll is handled electronically these days. It is the wise person who seeks and absorbs every bit of training available in these areas, because sooner or later, it will become an integral skill necessary for making a living no matter what career you choose.

CHAPTER 6

HOW MANY, HOW MUCH, AND HOW TO: RATERS AND PLANNERS

Loads do not appear on load boards randomly or by accident. Nor do the rates charged for hauling these loads pop up out of the clear blue sky. In the larger companies, there are people whose sole job is to take the loads booked by the marketing department and figure out how to disperse them. A second group figures out how much to charge for these loads. In smaller companies, the bookkeeper or dispatcher may also rate and plan loads in addition to dispatching duties.

THE PLANNER

The first position we'll study is the planner. These people are skilled in a science known as logistics. Usually, unless you have experience as a dispatcher or in marketing, you need a degree in transportation to become a planner for a major fleet. Getting a degree is usually the easiest way to start out since most modern shipping companies do not feel comfortable investing the time and money to train a person in logistics. And if they do, they will usually chose a person from inside the company operation to fill the position, most likely from the dispatching staff.

Like dispatching, planning is a job that seems simple on the surface, but it is far more complicated than appearances suggest. A planner's tools consist of a calendar; a working knowledge of the fleet of trucks the company operates; statistics about the driver, equipment capabilities, and average time factors for distance and for loading and unloading; an understanding of the idiosyncrasies of the company's customers; and a knack for planning for the unexpected.

Where a dispatcher sees individual loads and areas, the planner must see the "big" picture and use skill and judgment to ensure that enough trucks are placed or dispatched to heavy traffic areas during certain periods to cover all available loads. At the same time, the planner must be able to set up additional areas where marketing may have sold a load but the fleet usually doesn't operate, or where, due to the time of the year, growing seasons, or other factors, loads were not readily available. In a way, the planner must be able to consistently and accurately predict the future. Where and when will the next prime loading areas be, and how many drivers and rigs will it take to cover these loads?

Case Study

If we link the planner to the dispatcher, we can get a fair idea of what is entailed in the planner's job. Assume there are 10 dispatchers, each with 40 drivers in their "driver portfolio."

The dispatch has turned in load sheets—or, more likely, has registered them on the computer system. The load sheets for each driver state where they are, where they are destined, and whether they are empty or loaded.

Perhaps the planner sees there will soon be 70 drivers in the New England area, but also sees from the list of loads sold by marketing that there will only be 40 loads available by the time the 70 trucks arrive. A planner must make a number of decisions at this point. The options are many, but the consequences of each option must be weighed according to their profitability.

The first step it to notify marketing. Is there any chance of selling 30 more loads within a specific window of time? If the answer is yes, the planner divides the loads available between the 10 dispatchers, based on how many of each dispatchers' trucks will be in the region within that time period. In this example, each dispatcher will have one load for every two trucks heading into the region, but with a marketing prediction that more will be available within a short time.

If, however, marketing indicates that sales are slow in the region, the planner again studies the statistics presented. Are there drivers who live in the area, and are they due to some time off? If so, are they currently under loads that will lead them to the area? The planner now notifies the individual dispatchers who have these drivers in their portfolio. When these drivers call in, dispatch will ask if they want to go home. Or, dispatch may simply reassign loads, sometimes transferring a load from one truck to another while en route, in an effort to match needs.

At the same time, the planner notes that the company has a surplus of loads available in Texas, but almost none of the company trucks routed there. Another decision must be made.

Can the company route or profitably reroute rigs toward Texas to cover these loads, or do they notify the shippers that the dates they want the loads picked up may have to be changed, or do they offer the loads to another carrier at a discount on a trip-lease basis? None of these decisions is easy because the company's profitability rides on the planner's ability to set up a constantly moving picture of drivers, equipment, loads, destinations, and origins that involves the least amount of waiting or empty miles and a maximum of loaded, revenue-generating miles.

If it becomes obvious that enough trucks are available, if dispatch can convince enough drivers to stay on the road rather than going home for their day off, a message will be forwarded to dispatch to this effect. If it is impractical, and it looks as though the loads must be brokered, marketing may be notified. Or, the planner may call other carriers with whom the company has successfully brokered before to see if the Texas loads can be covered, and if there are loads available in the New England area for the anticipated empty trucks. In situations like these, trade-offs are very common. One company may trade their excess loads in one area for the other company's extra loads in another. Planning takes on the some of the aspects of the stock market as the picture unfolds. Risk, gamble, profit, and loss are all riding on these decisions. One mistake can cost the company thousands of dollars.

The Challenge of Planning

Some major headaches can pop up from day to day. Sales don't go through and have to be cancelled. Sometimes a major sale comes down from marketing that floods a certain area with loads or, when unloaded, floods a certain area with empty trucks. At times, the shippers miscalculate their product availability, leaving a truck and driver stuck in a location waiting for the product to become available. Planners have to have fairly thick skin; the circumstances of loads and load availability often mean that the planner will catch flak from both marketing and from drivers through dispatch.

If a planner does a good job setting up a load board, in theory, a dispatcher should be able to cover all the drivers and rigs in his or her portfolio within a 24-hour period and send them in directions that will promise brief waiting periods, or minimal deadhead miles between loads, or loads that will get a driver home in a timely fashion.

If, on the other hand, a planner does a poor job of setting up the load board, a company can end up with empty trucks all over the country, but none where the loads are, leaving drivers, dispatchers, and customers upset and unhappy. To make matters worse, such poor planning also means the company will lose money.

So far in our examples, the planner has been working with full truckloads of freight, which can be a reasonably complicated problem in itself. Now add in the factor of LTL (less-than-a-load) shipments, and the entire operation turns into nothing less than a gigantic jigsaw puzzle. Each piece must fit precisely, or the system will face problems. Not only must the planner figure out closest pickup and delivery points, he or she may also have to figure on en route pickup and delivery, and must know about the product itself. Five thousand pounds of steel ingots will not eat up the same amount of space on a trailer as five thousand pounds of rattan furniture. Planners deal in both weight and cubic feet. In the case of flatbed haulers, they deal in weight, height, over-dimensional products, and the number of feet of flatbed floor space the product will actually use. Perhaps the most valuable skills a planner possesses are a cool head under pressure and the ability to see problems in three dimensions. Planning is very much like a military general planning the strategy of troops about to go into battle or a chess master plotting three moves ahead.

THE RATER

Now let's look at what responsibility the rater handles. In a nutshell, the rater's responsibility is to see to it that the company charges enough for a load to make a reasonable profit, yet remains competitive enough to keep their customers from moving off to other carriers. A rater's work begins when marketing initially makes the sales call on the customer. The skills required of a good rater are an aptitude for math, the ability to figure complicated mathematics with a number of variable factors, and the ability to work closely with other people, primarily in planning and marketing. A rater is responsible for setting minimum rate figures for marketing to use as the absolute least amount the company could charge a customer for any given load.

At the same time, the rater must be aware of the laws that cover shipment of certain commodities because the deregulation of the trucking industry did not automatically cancel all government mandated rating schedules for certain shipments. Rating can become an intricate and complicated business, especially when you take into consideration the fact that many loads involve extra expenses, from special hauling permits to accessorial charges because of special handling difficulties.

Rates at one time were fully controlled by the federal government. Federal control was an effort to prevent large companies from low-balling, or undercutting, the loads of smaller companies. The fear was that undercutting would put the smaller firms out of business, thus creating a virtual monopoly in certain regions, on certain products, or in choice lanes of operation, called *power lanes.* Deregulation ended much of this federal control, and the results of deregulation were disastrous. Many small businesses were forced out of business, and a surprising number of major carriers became extinct as well. Deregulation led to a rating war. The result was predictable. Major haulers able to operate at as little as a penny a mile profit gobbled up their smaller competitors, driving rates down in the process. Many major haulers had banked on the idea that deregulation would never take place and, thinking themselves protected, overextended themselves or grew complacent in the belief that their hauling rights would make them virtually untouchable.

The price paid for deregulation was very high, and the industry is still staggering to lift itself free from the effects.

By law, a company must publish its rates for regulated freight and commodities, but even this is not as it seems. Trucking companies use discounts and other rating ploys to help lure business to them. Shippers are well aware of the practice and take full advantage of it. All this adds to the headaches a rater faces each day.

The same factors that affect a planner's day will have a hand in shaping a rater's day, plus a few more that don't enter the planner's realm at all. As an example, consider all those rigs heading into New England where the company currently has no loads. Marketing needs a tool to approach customers with to entice them to ship their commodities with the company, at least during this heavy traffic period. Marketing calls the rater and asks, "If we ship this load for ABC company at this price, can we make it work?" The rater has to do a fast bit of calculating because a customer is generally sitting across from the marketing representative waiting for an answer. If the answer is yes, marketing will try to confirm the load and send the rater and planner a set of dates for shipment and delivery, the amount of product to be handled, and any special needs or information that might affect the load or shipment.

TITLE AND EARNINGS

So far, we've treated the occupations of rater and planner as two separate jobs, and they usually are, especially in large companies. In smaller operations, however, a rater may also be the company bookkeeper, the planner, and may even handle call-in traffic to the terminal. Rating is a challenging, exciting, and often frustrating job, and it can lead to some of the higher executive positions within the company.

Planners and raters, again, do not start out with startlingly high salaries. Most begin around $18,000 and move up from there, but this is an area where executive training and grooming takes place, and for the upwardly mobile, it is an excellent starting point. Most companies prefer college trained individuals for these jobs, but if you can demonstrate some solid math skills, you may have a shot at the position without a degree.

CHAPTER 7

DO WE HAVE A DEAL?

Do you like people? Are you challenged by competition? Do you have a good telephone presence, and are you able to sit across the desk from a business executive and represent yourself and your company with confidence? Are you aggressive about success? Then you may have what it takes to enter *marketing.*

As explained earlier, the trucking industry is a vast operation, and the departments within a trucking company are interdependent. Without drivers, the trucks stand still. Without profit and organization, the business fails. Without loads, the drivers have nothing to haul. Marketing's job is to sell the company's services to its clients. Marketing is the sales arm of the company team.

DUTIES AND QUALIFICATIONS

Once again, this is an occupation that isn't for everyone. While it is not absolutely necessary to have specific education to enter marketing, most of the larger operations are looking for men and women who have studied subjects such as logistics, business administration, business management, and commercial marketing. Yet, classes alone do not suffice to fully train someone for the specific and often unusual demands that arise within the commercial trucking world.

A marketing or sales representative calls on producers, agents, manufacturers, and businesses who ship or receive commodities of every description from every corner of the world. It is a good bet that as you read this chapter, the items you are wearing, using, and surrounded by came to you because of the trucking industry and were delivered only after the successful efforts of a marketing representative for a transportation company. Each of these everyday items—from the light bulb in your desk lamp to the threads in your clothing—was probably shipped by truck. Someone had to sell the manufacturer the services of that trucking firm. That someone was a marketing or sales representative.

The duties of the sales rep are the same no matter where they are employed, but the methods salespeople use to do the job vary. Some never leave their office, but spend most of their day on the phone calling clients and setting up load schedules. It is more common, however, for marketing reps to physically call upon their prospective clients. They will make appointments to meet shippers just as any salesperson would. The biggest skill a marketing representative can bring to his or her job is the ability to listen and understand the needs and desires of the client and the imagination and skills to solve problems and meet those needs.

MAKING THE SALE

Interviews with marketing professionals reveal a few surprising facts. First, although price is a major tool in a sales rep's arsenal, it is not always the primary reason shippers select a specific company to handle their trucking needs. After deregulation, many trucking firms jumped into areas they had never serviced before. Too many were ill equipped to service their new clients and their specific needs, even though they quoted low prices for these services. The end result was that in today's trucking market, price is but one factor a shipper considers before contracting with a trucking firm.

One of the biggest concerns is on-time delivery. Marketing representatives must know the strengths and weaknesses of their company, the various areas in which the company operates, and, to some extent, the strengths and weaknesses of the rival companies vying for the client's shipping business. Some of the geographic areas served by the firm may be serviced on a regular schedule. Often these areas of operation are called *power lanes*. At any given time, the company will always have units in various stages of their route on the power lanes—from loading to unloading to in-transit. And the company always has loads available at each end of the route. Power lanes are direct, high-speed, quick turnaround routes, such as New York to Chicago. A good marketing rep will use the company's power lanes to the shipper's and the firm's advantage.

Perhaps this sounds complicated, so let's look at a power lane in action. ABC Trucking operates in all 48 states, specializing in refrigerated shipments of meat. They have a client in

Denver who ships six loads a week to New York and a shipper in New Jersey who ships nine truckloads of imported meat to Omaha every week. The marketing rep for ABC finds that a packing company in Cheyenne, Wyoming, consistently ships four loads of meat a week to a processor in Albany, New York.

A good rep will use this knowledge, combined with the knowledge of ABC's power lanes, to propose a contract that will benefit both the Cheyenne packer and ABC Trucking. As you can see from this example, the rep has an excellent chance not only of gaining the business of the Cheyenne client, but also of picking up the remaining East Coast shipments for ABC on the other end of the power lane. Negotiating the terms of this contract are very much like guaranteeing the company's continued existence for whatever the contract term might be.

The marketing rep must have an excellent grasp of operating costs, especially if he or she works for a smaller firm in which the staff may "wear more than one hat." He or she may be the rater as well as the marketing rep and has to know, at least approximately, the costs of any operations. The company's survival and their customers' satisfaction rests on this knowledge and ability.

Many trucking companies maintain offices or terminals throughout the country or along their main power lanes. Most of these offices are staffed by dispatchers and marketing reps. A representative may only see the main office once or twice a year and has to be able to operate independently with minimal supervision. In a sense, this position and the accompanying responsibility is much like that which a driver faces. Although it may sound fun to work without the boss peering over your shoulder, it's a heavy responsibility to know that the success of the operation rests on your ability to "read" a shipper and understand what is required, and your ability to close a sale.

COLLECTION AND CUSTOMER SERVICE

One major drawback with the position can be collection. Some companies have specialists who handle accounts; others depend on their sales force to collect the fees from their individual clients. It's a sad fact of life that not all companies or individuals pay their bills on time, and when this happens, someone holds the responsibility of collecting these overdue accounts. Collection is very often one of the duties of a marketing rep. The reasoning is fairly obvious. The salesperson knows the company and the individual personally, and should possess the necessary tact to collect the funds due without incurring the anger or resentment of the customer.

The reverse is also true. Often, if there is a problem with a shipment, the first one a shipper calls is the marketing rep. Why? Because the marketing rep usually is the only person the customer deals with personally within the trucking company, except, perhaps, for the driver. Rather than call a main office, which may be thousands of miles away, the shipper calls the marketing rep looking for answers or redress on a shipment problem.

The amount of power actually vested in a marketing representative varies from company to company. In some firms, the rep may be able to settle claims independently. In others, he or she may simply be a salesperson whose responsibility and problem-solving abilities stop when the contract to ship is signed. Other marketing reps may have powers somewhere in between these extremes.

EARNINGS

Just as duties and responsibilities vary, wages can be paid in a number of ways. The most common is a base salary and a commission schedule. Commission is a percentage paid the salesperson for each shipment booked or each signed contract brought in. In addition, some reps may receive certain bonuses, usually for attracting and keeping new shippers. Expense accounts are fairly common, especially within the larger corporations, primarily because of travel and the extra costs it involves, such as taking a client out to lunch and paying for hotel stays and similar business expenses. Company cars are also fairly common, especially with the larger companies. It's not unusual for representatives with large territories to accumulate enough mileage in a year to make them feel as though they rival truck drivers.

Commission payments can take a variety of forms, but two basic payment systems are common. In the first, the marketing representative receives a basic wage and does not receive commission until he or she reaches a set number of sales or contracts, or a specific dollar amount. Then, any percentage booked over that base amount is subject to commission.

The second method, which is becoming less common, is a draw against commission, where the marketing rep's skills are tested to the maximum. Although the representative receives a basic salary, it is a draw against the minimum amount he or she is expected and required to sell. Drawing against commission is a risky way of making a living unless you are very, very good at what you do. Yet, the biggest advantage is the fact that companies who pay in this way are shouldering a minimal risk, and they are less inclined to demand that marketing representatives provide educational or experience credentials before being hired. A seasoned, professional marketing representative is a "hot" commodity, sought after by many companies. He or she has no need to assume the risk of straight commission. A "green" marketing rep may have to prove himself or herself, and a straight commission position may be all that's readily available. It is one way to break into the business and discover for yourself whether or not you are cut out for it.

As for actual income, marketing representatives enjoy a challenging and unique position in that they literally are responsible for the ceiling on their earnings. Because the primary source of their income is commission, the more sales they make and the more contracts they produce, the more they earn. That's why you will see the most successful marketing reps living in nice homes, wearing nice clothes, and driving nice cars. The average income of a marketing representative varies widely according to the method of payment, geographic location, and the sales skills of the rep. The average starting wage for a sales representative is around $25,000 per year, and top professional sales representatives in the transportation industry may earn well over $100,000.

In addition to base salaries and/or commission, it is becoming more and more common to set a sales goal—usually on an annual basis—and to offer an incentive if the sales representative exceeds that goal. Since this excess amounts to what might be considered pure profit, bonuses for surpassing these sales goals can be quite lavish. Some companies offer exotic trips, automobiles, or an annual cash bonus.

HAZARDS OF SALES

As with most good things, there is a price to be paid if your intent is to maintain the lifestyle of a successful marketing rep. The first price is time. Few marketing representatives work an actual nine-to-five schedule, or even an eight-hour day. They are in their offices early, setting appointments, usually for later in the week or month. Then they leave on appointments they set earlier. No matter how each sales call goes, whether successful or not, the rep has to face the next client full of enthusiasm, concern, and energy. It's hard to keep smiling when you've been turned down by every person you've called on that day, but that's what a marketing representative must do. This confidence that good things happen to people who work hard and enthusiastically is part of a salesperson's philosophy, and if you are easily discouraged or depressed, if you become angered or upset easily, marketing is definitely not the career for you.

Life for a marketing representative tends to be fast paced and loaded with pressure. This is the sort of career that can create ulcers and age you fast, if you let it. Stress is another price a marketing representative must be willing to pay. The challenge of setting and making appointments; discovering and capitalizing on the needs of the clients; scheduling, quoting, and confirming sales; and creating booking contracts fills a sales representative's day. While he or she may arrive at the office at 7 A.M., and spend an entire day calling on prospects, evening may find the salesperson back in the office, long after everyone else has gone home, going over contract terms, pricing, following up on calls that came in during the day, and even making phone calls to other firms in different time zones. Often the final meal of the day is fast food gulped down with a phone in one hand and some client's contract out on the desk. It is a career for someone who is incurably competitive. Often, people who make the best marketing professionals were highly competitive in sports activities in school.

Many firms look at their sales representatives as public relations people and tend to expect their marketing personnel to take a personal interest in the clients they call upon. In a sense, this is a form of office politics, and in the marketing game, you either play by the rules or find another profession. This means that at times a marketing person may have to show up for events sponsored by an important client, perhaps spend a weekend tending to details of a client's contract, and, very often, approach the client when shipping rates must be raised to remain profitable. In short, the marketing representative is the link between his or her company and the shipper. If the link is weak, both the trucking firm and the shipper tend to suffer.

ADVANTAGES IN MARKETING

If a person wishes to gain executive status, the marketing avenue is another excellent career path to follow. It provides the vital experience needed within the administration of any major company. A marketing representative learns the needs and necessary operating basics of the clients the company serves, and at the same time, he or she learns the basics of the day-to-day operations of the trucking company. This broad spectrum of knowledge is a prerequisite to moving up within the ranks of the business successfully.

Today's modern technology has added an entirely new wrinkle to the field within the trucking industry. Even though there is nothing new about import items, satellite technology and rapidly expanding international businesses have created a situation of new opportunities. For instance, in 1989, Mayflower signed a contract with the Soviet Union for their international moving and certain freight trade. More and more companies are entering into contracts and agreements between U.S.-based transportation companies and foreign-based manufacturers and services. In the future, the trend may well be toward bilingual marketing personnel who will be responsible for setting up foreign transportation contract negotiations.

Finally, if a marketing representative eventually wanted to move away from the transportation industry, the skills that are developed and honed as a marketing rep for a trucking firm are easily applicable to any other business that employs people who need to represent and sell their company's products or services to other people or businesses. Marketing skills, whether they are applied to trucking or any other industry, are in great demand, and those who can handle the pressure and responsibility of marketing can carve an excellent career for themselves.

CHAPTER 8

YOUR FAULT, MY FAULT, NO FAULT

How many times have you gone to the store, picked up a dozen eggs, then, before you carried them to the checkout counter, peeked inside to make sure none were broken? Most of us have, probably after an unfortunate experience with eggs on a previous shopping trip. It's a normal precaution to make sure the item we intend to buy is intact and useful. This applies to everything from eggs to automobiles. Within the trucking industry, there is a career position that deals with precisely this sort of problem. That career is inside the claims department.

THE CLAIMS PROCESSOR

If you imagine yourself in the role of referee in a ball game, you can grasp the basics of claims. However, it's important to keep in mind that you are an employee of a trucking firm, and each claim you settle in favor of a shipper represents a loss to your company. Yet, there's more to it than that. Your first and foremost task is to try to see to it that claims are prevented before they can happen.

By definition, a *claim* is a demand for compensation for damages done, either to the product or to the company's relationship with its customers. In other words, nothing has to actually break to warrant a claim. The most common non-physical damage claim in the trucking business occurs because of late deliveries. If a product is broken in shipment, the settlement is fairly simple, but what if a shipper's business is hurt because of a late delivery to a client? What is that worth? What is the price tag for a shipper's reputation? As you can see, claim settlements can be very simple or extremely complicated.

There is also the question of responsibility. Consider oranges. Oranges are picked as they reach their peak. Once the harvest begins, time becomes the enemy because oranges, like any citrus fruit, remain fresh only so long, then begin to lose their market appeal. Once picked, they are hauled from the orchard to be crated. The crates are stacked on pallets and placed on a loading dock to be picked up. Finally, the oranges are picked up by a truck and hauled to their destination. When they arrive, they are inspected, either by a company official or a trained inspector. If the inspector determines that the oranges have passed beyond ripeness and are no longer fit to be served or sold, they are sent to a pulper to become juice, as are most damaged citrus fruits. At this point, a claim may—and almost certainly will—be filed.

The question now is, who is responsible for the damage in this case? Is it the people who picked the oranges? Did they wait too long? Is it the people who packed or crated the oranges? Did the load wait too long before being handled, or was it left out in the hot Florida or California sunshine too long? Was it the trucker's fault? Did the trucker fail to refrigerate the load or set the thermostat improperly? In the business world, if damage occurs, someone faces a loss, and no one willingly accepts this responsibility.

Claims people are part complaint department, part detective, part referee, part negotiator, and, in some ways, they are part hall monitor. If too many claims come in from one trucker's loads, one type of shipment, or one shipper, a claims processor must not only settle the claim, but must act fast to determine why the damage has taken place and then take the steps necessary to prevent it from happening again, especially if it proves to be the trucking company who is at fault.

Job Requirements and Training

Training for a claims processor is varied. At one extreme, a claims processor may need a working knowledge of the laws governing transportation. On the other hand, the requirements may be simpler: just a good phone manner and the ability to communicate and handle simple mathematics. The majority of claims people, however, begin and learn on the job because there are few better ways to learn this sometimes complicated business. Other skill requirements may include word processor or computer knowledge, general office skills such as filing and typing, a knowledge of insurance, and above-average skills in math and deductive reasoning.

Finally, a claims processor, at times, needs to be a bit hard-nosed. Often you will find yourself the bearer of bad news. Imagine yourself telling drivers that the damage to their last load was their fault, and the company is going to charge them for it. Imagine telling a shipper that his or her product was improperly packaged, and therefore, the damage done it was not the company's fault. Some people have no problem with this kind of confrontation; others never do work up the courage or nerve to handle the job.

TWO CASE STUDIES

Often, a claims processor must put together the pieces of a claim like a puzzle, employ a great deal of general knowledge, and know where to go to learn specifics on certain products. Sound complicated? It often is. Here are examples of two actual claims and what was required of the claims person before they could be settled.

Florida Oranges

Trucker A picked up a load of oranges in Florida in October destined for Des Moines, Iowa. When the trucker arrived, the fruit was "probed"—a method of measuring the temperature of the fruit by inserting a thermometer probe into one of the oranges buried deep within the crate—and the shipper rejected the load as "hot." The warm temperatures inside the oranges indicated that the fermentation process was about to begin. This meant that the oranges would not enjoy a long shelf life in any grocery store, and therefore they were useless to the grocery supplier to whom they were shipped. The entire load was rejected and sent to the pulpers at a major loss to the shipper. In a case like this, the driver should call his or her company's claims department, before even leaving the loading dock, and explain the situation. Half the battle of settling claims is to receive the information about a potentially damaged load as soon as possible.

In this case, the shipper claimed the trucking company was responsible, accusing the driver of not setting the refrigeration thermostat at the right setting. The driver argued that the thermostat was set correctly and that the oranges probably sat on the dock too long before being shipped. Who was right?

Photos and samples taken from the load were sent to the claims department. A thin, blue, hair-like growth was observed on the skin of the fruit. The claims processor called the local university and talked with an expert before making a decision in favor of the trucking company. How? The blue hair-like substance was the beginning stages of mold. The university people told the claims processor the amount of time needed for an orange to reach the stage where mold begins to form. Then, by figuring the amount of time between pick up and delivery, the processor was able to determine that the fermentation process had already begun before the driver ever loaded the oranges.

A Broken Table

The second claim involved furniture. A driver had picked up a load from a military family moving from Missouri to Texas. When moving furniture, it is a common practice to disassemble some items in order to protect them and, at the same time, to save space on the trailer. In this case, the driver disassembled a dining table whose base consisted of a type of particleboard, a fairly common building material in less expensive furniture. When the load arrived in Texas, the family found that the screws that held the table legs to the particleboard table could no longer be tightened. The holes had stripped out. The table was unusable and had to be repaired. The question was, did the moving company owe for damage to the table, or should the customer take responsibility?

A claims processor studied the situation, then questioned both the driver and the customer. Had the table been disassembled by movers and shipped before? The answer was "yes." How many times? Twice, prior to this move. Then the claims processor asked if the driver had noted on the load sheets that the table was particleboard, and that the legs were removed. The driver said "no." The table was listed, but not in so specific a manner. The claims processor decided in favor of the customer, but only because the driver failed to write the table up on the load sheet as being constructed of particleboard. During the investigation, the claims processor learned from manufacturers that particleboard is used in construction because it's cheap, but that removing and replacing screws in the table base would tend to weaken the binding compound—a mixture of wood chips and glue—that holds the particles together. In this case, multiple moves and repeated disassembly had weakened it until the screws threads no longer had anything to grip.

A claims processor is a detail person, an organized person. Nothing escapes his or her notice. A claims processor may, from time to time, work hand in hand with insurance companies if products are damaged during an accident.

Indeed, part of the claims person's job is very similar to an insurance adjuster's duties.

In a sense, a claims person is the trucking company's complaint department. At the same time, the claims person is the driver's friend or foe, depending on whether the driver is found to be at fault for a claim or if it's a product problem that caused the damage. It takes a very special type of person to work this position because no matter how the claim turns out, someone is going to wind up unhappy over the outcome.

WHO PAYS FOR CLAIMS?

This is an excellent place to address who, exactly, pays for a claim. Obviously, if the damage to the goods is the fault of the shipper, the shipper must stand the loss. However, if it's the trucking company's fault, one of three things can happen. First, the company may decide, on the advice of the claims processor, to "eat" the loss themselves, to pay for it and not charge the driver. Usually this will happen when the claims processor has determined that, while the shipper cannot be held liable, either there was no reasonable way the driver could have foreseen the possibility of damage, or there was nothing the driver could have done to prevent it.

The second possibility is that the damage will be charged to the driver. If this happens, it is because the claims processor feels the driver was negligent in his or her duties and could have prevented the damage had the job been done properly.

The third possibility, and probably the most common, is that the company and the driver will share the blame. In some companies—especially household moving operations—the driver has set obligations that resemble insurance. If a claim runs $100, the driver may have to pay 25 percent of the cost—in this case, $25—up to a maximum amount per shipment of perhaps $200. One exception is lost or missing articles. Should part of the load turn up missing, the driver is generally required to stand the total cost of the claim. That's the main reason most drivers are very careful about tallying up the number of boxes, crates, pallets, or items of cargo. It doesn't take too many missing items to completely destroy a paycheck.

Claims are never taken lightly. Because of this, the claims person carries a heavy responsibility. One of the most difficult areas of claims work is claims settlements due to accidents. Even as the insurance company and its investigators are working the claim that comes from a traffic accident, the claims processor is assessing how much, if any, of the load can be salvaged and whether it did, in fact, suffer any damage. Then, in cooperation with the other divisions within the company, the claims department works at getting that portion of the shipment that is salvageable picked up and delivered. In some companies, drivers are given the home phone numbers of claims persons, or a claims representative is on duty 24-hours a day, seven days a week, just to make sure any potential problems are addressed immediately.

CLAIMS MADE BY TRUCKING FIRMS

So far, we've only discussed claims owed customers of the company. Yet, there is another type of claim: one made by the trucking company itself. By law, a driver, the driver's equipment, and the company's time are all worth money. At times, shippers find themselves owing a claim for delaying a driver and the driver's equipment.

This type of claim is illustrated in the following incident. Driver A was dispatched to ABC Company in Dallas. As usual, the driver was given an appointment time to be at the loading dock. In this case, the truck was due at 6 A.M. on Wednesday. The driver showed up on time, only to discover that the company had suffered a problem with some of its manufacturing equipment and the product was not yet ready to be loaded. ABC Company had not bothered to call the driver's company to tell them of the delay. The driver called dispatch and was then put in contact with the claims department to inform them of the situation. The manufacturer did not start loading the driver's truck until 8:30 the next morning. When loading was completed, the driver called the terminal and once again reported to the claims processor. The manufacturer was charged a hundred dollars an hour for the driver and the company's equipment for waiting time. In this particular example, the specific rates for waiting time are published, and the circumstances under which these fees can be charged are very clear. It's the claims person's job to know when and where to apply these rules and what the fees are.

In trucking, just as in any other business, time is money. This type of claim is reasonably easy to understand. Assume the payments on the tractor and trailer amount to $3,500 per month, licensing and permits are $7,000 a year, and insurance is $5,000 a year. The driver's wage is 32 cents per mile to translate to $18 an hour, plus the cost of simply eating and sleeping while out on the highway. Add all these expenses, plus the cost of not being loaded and running and earning, and a hundred dollar an hour charge can actually seem reasonable.

The claims processor's word is not always final, and this, too, goes with the position. In some cases, customers simply refuse to believe that damage was the fault of their people, their product, or anything within the sphere of their control. When all other avenues have been exhausted, it sometimes happens that the trucking firm and the customer find themselves in a court of law. This is why it is so urgently important that a claims person is exacting in his or her work. What may have seemed a routine claim at the time could evolve into a court case if the person being assessed the claim disagrees.

EARNINGS

The claims person can expect to earn only a mediocre wage at the beginning of a career. Yet, as experience is gained, the wages climb, and the work is extremely steady. The average starting wage usually runs around $15,000 to $20,000, unless an associate's degree in transportation law is expected, and this is a fairly rare requirement.

Claims tends to be a highly specialized area, but one direction a claims person can aspire to is customer service and some of the administrative posts within the company. These, in turn, can lead into major employment areas within the trucking industry.

CHAPTER 9

MAY WE SEE YOUR PAPERS?

Some jobs are born from the expansion of businesses and other because of new technology. But a career in *rights and permits* comes directly from the red tape that only government is capable of creating. Moreover, rights and permits are a highly specialized aspect of the trucking industry.

THE BASIC CONCEPT

To illustrate this, assume you are going on vacation, and your neighbor asks you to drop a package off with a friend in another state. And, to make up for the hassle, your neighbor gives you tickets to a ball game as a kind of payment. You would probably place the package in your car and drive away, without a second thought. If you did this with a truck, you would be operating illegally.

In the trucking business, you need to have state and federal permission to deliver the package. You must also have published rates so your competitors have a fair chance of competing with you. You must not only have the rights, or authority, that specifically state that you can carry whatever the package contains, but that you can carry it through the states where you will travel, as well. Your truck must be licensed in its state of registration, and you may also need permits for the fuel it will consume and the miles it will travel through each state or province on the way.

If this sounds a little far-fetched to you, or even a bit unfair in a democratic country, you aren't alone. The trucking industry for years has fought the idea of individual permits and, to a lesser extent, the idea of rights and authorities dictated by federal and state government. In fact, back in 1951, trucking companies and associations took out full-page ads in magazines and newspapers telling the public of their dilemma because it was the public's opinion that freight rates were rising simply because trucking companies were greedy. Yet, despite these protests, it is unlikely the practice will ever end.

For one thing, there is revenue to consider. Millions of dollars come into individual states and to the federal government each year from permits and fees assessed trucks. It is highly unlikely that the states will voluntarily relinquish this income; nor is the federal government known for turning loose of any of its revenue-producing entities.

An Example

It's extremely hard to grasp the concept of rights, authority, and permits. As an example, let's turn once more to our old friend, the orange. The federal government says that oranges, in their natural state, are an exempt commodity. This means trucking companies do not need federally issued authority or rights to haul them. Many raw foodstuff items fall into this classification. However, if a truck is loaded with oranges in Florida and hauls them north through Georgia, the state of Georgia requires a stamp—called an *exempt hauler's permit*—granting permission, for a small fee, to haul exempt items through the state. The cost of the stamp is minimal, about $5. However, should a truck be caught in Georgia hauling exempt commodities such as oranges without the stamp, the fine can be as high as $500. In other words, even though it is federally legal to haul exempt commodities—in this example, oranges—a state may arbitrarily make it illegal when the truck crosses their boundary. The rule governing this applies throughout the legal structure of the trucking business. Federal law supercedes state law, unless the state law is more stringent than the original federal mandate.

One conflict between federal and state laws occurred when the federal government raised the maximum legal weight limit from 73,280 pounds to 80,000 pounds. The states of Illinois and Missouri refused to accept the new weight legislation. The result was that legally loaded trucks would hit these state borders and be slapped with fines the minute they touched a Missouri or Illinois scale. To avoid these fines, trucks literally had to detour around two states to reach their destination. This was one of the few cases where the federal government stepped in and threatened to reduce or withhold federal highway funds if the states did not bring their laws into line with their neighbors. These states were, in fact, holding the trucking industry hostage, especially if their routes followed I-70 or I-80, two major east/west interstate highways.

But the federal government is fully capable of clouding its own legal waters. Again, our old friend, the orange, makes an excellent example. If the oranges are taken to a pulper, such as the Donald Duck orange juice facility near Lakeland, Florida, the oranges are no longer exempt. The truck must have federal rights or authority to haul the oranges in juice form out of the state of Florida. The product is still oranges, but the law states that in concentrate or liquid form, the oranges are no longer exempt.

LICENSING

Everyone is familiar with licensing. Most likely, you have a car, and you know that before you can legally operate your car on the street, it must be licensed. This is true of trucks, as well. The primary license—called a *base plate*—is the license plate of the state where the truck is registered. The base plate is not recognized beyond the boundaries of the state of issuance unless the state has a reciprocity agreement with other states. Reciprocity simply means that states exchange the right to operate within each other's borders.

If a truck is licensed in Iowa, it does not have the right to operate in Illinois because Illinois does not have a reciprocity agreement with Iowa. This means that an Iowa truck crossing into Illinois must either hold an Illinois permit or must buy a temporary 72-hour permit at a state weigh station before it is allowed to legally cross through Illinois. The penalties for not obtaining this permit can be very severe. In Illinois, for example, the permit costs about $25. If, however, the permit expires, and the truck is still inside the state and is caught, the fine is the price of an Illinois base plate, or about $1,500. Obviously no company can afford that kind of expense for very long. To prevent it, the permit department makes sure the driver knows that he or she must pick up an Illinois temporary permit, or must have an Illinois permit in the truck's permit portfolio.

Each truck operating in an interstate manner must have various permits, authorities, and licenses. Usually these are kept inside the truck in a large book similar to a photo album, or they are affixed to the cab of the truck in specific locations. Permit stickers and books must be presented whenever state authorities ask to see them.

Once again, the computer age is rapidly invading even this aspect of trucking. While the need for state permits has not changed, the old cab decal/sticker and permit book packed with official bits of paper and stamps is rapidly giving way to a single sheet listing the truck's DOT number and a list of the states it is authorized to operate in, all accessible by computer at state ports of entry and weigh staions. In fact, even the weigh station can be handled electronically with an on-board device that allows a busy weigh station to "green light" a truck and allow it to bypass the scale whose loaded weight is registered electronically via a small transponder mounted in the truck.

Still, the operator must stand ready to produce the documents to officials.

Revenue for Road Maintenance

In the early days of the industry, there were no permits to worry about, but as more and more trucks appeared on the road, states began to view commercial haulers as a source of both expense and revenue. The expense viewpoint is based on the belief that a vehicle weighing eighty thousand pounds or so must be doing more damage to roadways than a four thousand–pound passenger car. This argument is only partially true since there are far more passenger vehicles traveling the nation's highways than trucks. In addition, some highways and roads are restricted to passenger vehicles only and are still breaking down as rapidly as nonregulated roads. However, no one can deny that the heavy haulers do create their share of road damage.

One of the truly angry arguments offered by the trucking industry concerning the use of the interstate road system is based on the fact that these roads were not always called interstates. Their true name is the National Defense Highway System, and the federal government originally built these concrete super highways so that in times of war or emergency trucks would be able to haul loads of up to 100,000 pounds across the country at high speeds with a minimum of delay. The roads were to be built to handle this type of stress, but they obviously have not. The interstate system has been deteriorating much faster than expected. And the trucking industry has been forced to pay the lion's share of the upkeep for state and national highways through increased fuel taxes, special fuel permits, and more. Anyone who expects to enter the industry can expect to hear the complaints that accompany this taxation. But, like complaints about the weather, in reality, there is very little that can, or ever will, be done about the situation.

State Fees

Over the past decade, there have been a number of moves to "federalize" licensing for heavy over-the-road vehicles, but each attempt has been blocked by states. However, the income generated by the trucking industry on a state-by-state basis is so high that it is extremely unlikely that states will ever lose control of truck licensing. State and federal regulation seem here to stay. And this, in turn, means that those who handle permits and authority for trucking firms have very secure jobs.

For some states, this method of taxing a truck is aimed at forcing the trucking operation to do retail business within the state's boundaries. For example, most truckers know that if they are running west through Mississippi, heading for Texas, once they reach Texas, the fuel prices will drop dramatically. The state imposes fewer user taxes on its fuel. Obviously this means that Mississippi does not sell as much fuel to truckers as Texas does.

To combat this problem, Mississippi created a permit system that penalizes a truck for not fueling within state borders. It's a system based on the number of miles the truck travels through the state. If the driver does not buy fuel, when he or she crosses the last weigh station before exiting Mississippi, a fee based on the number of miles traveled is assessed against the truck and must be paid before the driver is allowed to leave the state. If, on the other hand, the driver had taken on at least the minimum amount of fuel required to satisfy the state requirements at a legitimate Mississippi fueling station, no fee is charged, and the truck is allowed to proceed.

This system of revenue earnings exists in a wide variety of ways. In Ohio, for instance, a trucker must possess a permit called an *Ohio HUT.* HUT stands for Highway User Tax. Each quarter of the year, the truck's mileage while operating within Ohio borders must be reported and a fee paid based on those miles. One highway is exempt from this fee and that's the toll road that traverses the state from east to west. The truck is not liable for any mileage taxes as long as it remains on the Ohio Turnpike. Of course, the truck is assessed a major fee for the right to travel the toll road, so one way or another, the state does manage to collect from the trucking industry.

In Utah, on the other hand, a truck cannot buy fuel unless it has a Utah fuel permit. When a fuel purchase is made, the permit number is recorded on the sales receipt that is forwarded to the state tax division, and trucks are either taxed or refunded accordingly.

Fees paid by trucks are not always aimed at maintaining highways. In Texas, for instance, truckers must buy and carry a Texas Railroad Commission stamp, along with their Texas permit. This money is used to help maintain the railways and enhance rail service within the state. In other words, the trucking industry is taxed to help support one of its biggest competitors. If all this sounds confusing, or perhaps unfair, keep in mind that there are 49 continental states, all the Canadian provinces, and even some of the Mexican states to consider, each with its own set of rules and regulations. We've only discussed a small part of the large, complex permit system.

CANADIAN RIGHTS AND PERMITS

Rights, permits, and authority are not just a product of the United States. Trucks crossing into Canada from the United States or operating from Canadian provinces and across national boundaries face the same requirements. In addition, trucks are subject to certain inspections at the borders, and if the proper permits or licenses are not displayed, the truck may either be turned away or forced to pay a rather high fee for the right to cross the boundary. For trucks hauling exempt commodities, or produce of any sort, an additional fee may be assessed. This pays for an inspection process to legalize certain products—usually products consumers will eventually eat—as these products cross international boundaries.

Inside Canada, trucks must maintain an additional set of permits for operating inside each of the Canadian provinces, which is not so very different from requirements in the United States. Trucks operating in Canada are expected to conform to Canadian laws and rules, just as Canadian trucks operating in the United States are expected to maintain the proper U.S. permits, licenses, and documentation. Even equipment rules may vary. For instance, no lights are required on the tractor mirrors on the U.S. side of the border, but at least one province in Canada requires an amber marker light on the back side of the mirror mount for a truck to legally operate on the highways.

In addition, a loaded truck entering or leaving Canada must either have a broker, or post a *bond*—a major amount of money—before it is allowed to cross the boundary. In essence, the broker, which is a Canadian business when entering the

Canadian provinces, and a U.S. business when coming into the United States, is guaranteeing that the load is a legal commodity, has a legitimate business destination, that the product is actually being purchased (which means taxes and duties will be paid), that all international paperwork is in order, and more or less acts as a sponsor for the truck and its load.

THE RIGHTS AND PERMITS WORKER

An individual working within the rights and permits division of a trucking firm can expect to face countless details. In addition to keeping track of when and how each tax or fee is to be handled, anyone working this division must also keep up with the constantly changing requirements of each state in which the company's trucks operate. It is a position of extremely high responsibility, requiring excellent math skills and tremendous organizational talents. One mistake can cost the company thousands of dollars. And just to keep things interesting, state and federal requirements are constantly changing, so what is legal this week may no longer be acceptable the next. If you like variety in your life and the element of surprise, you'll love working in the permit department.

The cost of maintaining permits for a truck traveling cross-country averages around $7,000 and is going up constantly. Therefore, if you work for a company and have 20 trucks to maintain licensing, fees, rights, and permits for, you are responsible for a minimum of $140,000 worth of documentation. As you have already seen, failure to maintain the proper permit or license can be excessively expensive.

At the same time, although the responsibility usually is assigned to the safety department, you will find that rights and permits people must also make sure that the trucks and the drivers are able to pass individual state inspections. California, for instance, makes spot-check inspections of trucks crossing into or operating within their boundaries. If the vehicle can't pass inspection, it is tagged out of service and not allowed to operate again, or to purchase the proper operating permits, until it has satisfied the inspection requirements.

Finally, the permit department is usually entrusted with insurance coverage as well. Not only is separate insurance required when operating a truck outside of its national boundaries, but some states—Kansas, for example—require special insurance coverage for trucks operating in the state of Oregon, which requires a special statement of insurance before trucks are allowed to enter. It is the permit department's job to see that this insurance is in effect when the truck leaves the terminal.

Training

If all this seem overwhelming, don't worry. While it is extremely complicated, and even state authorities sometimes are unsure of what is and is not proper, no company is going to throw you into the fray untrained and unprepared.

This is one area where a college degree may not be required, although it may prove necessary later as you move up the corporate ladder. Unless you study transportation law, permits is such a specialized area that many, if not most, companies prefer to train their personnel themselves.

Not only can you expect some training from the company, you can also rely on each state to supply you with information. Each state offers specific guidelines for operation within their boundaries, and usually these guidelines are sent or explained when you file the request for a permit. In addition, when state legislatures change the rules or laws governing commerce within their boundaries, the state is usually fairly quick to send an update to companies that regularly operate in their area. The trick is to keep up with the changes and requirements.

Earnings

Wages for people working permits, authority, and licensing vary according to how many trucks the company operates and how many states they operate in. The wage scale runs the gamut from very low—perhaps $8.50 an hour—to near-professional level wages in excess of $35,000 per year. Once again, it is easy to move up from this position, to areas such as bookkeeping, safety, planning, and others.

One more thing should be noted, as well. This is one area of the business that, like driving, can offer a way to become self-employed. People who are experienced and skilled in handling authority requests, licensing, rights, and permits often set themselves up as consultants, selling their services and skills to a number of companies at a time. This can be an extremely lucrative business and, as long as individual states continue to operate on their own, one that shows no signs of weakening or fading away.

CHAPTER 10

MAKING IT BIG IN OIL

Trucks have five to sixteen or more, forward gears; twin, interlockable differentials; multiplate clutches; and electronically monitored and metered fuel injection systems. They may be turbo-charged, blown, or naturally aspirated. In other words, the mechanics of a truck are complicated. To keep them operating efficiently and safely, trucks must be maintained on a regular basis.

Maintenance is one area that is changing more rapidly than any other aspect of the industry. Rigs are becoming increasingly complicated and more and more dependent on electronic technology. Many companies are leasing rather than purchasing their rigs, and those that are purchasing are buying extended warranties. With these changes, a division between trucking operations is beginning to form.

IN-HOUSE SHOPS

At one time, almost all carriers employed their own shop, with their own full-service mechanics. Today, many companies that once depended on an all-purpose, in-house diesel mechanic for all repairs are shifting toward an individual dedicated to simply maintaining the vehicle, while leaving the high-tech and heavy-duty mechanical repair to the dealerships.

At the same time, some carriers are looking at the enormous expense of purchasing new equipment and opting instead to continue to maintain their own. These firms are hiring full-line mechanics to meet their needs. Most companies with full-service shops today run a split fleet of company trucks and owner/operators. While the shop also services company-owned equipment, much of the revenue generated to pay shop expenses is earned from servicing owner/operator trucks, whose drivers pay for the maintenance.

This dual direction works in the favor of anyone interested in mechanics and maintenance. The field is expanding and more and more, especially in the bigger shops, specialization is beginning to take place. At the same time, vocational/technical schools across the country are teaching skills that can readily be applied within the framework of almost any shop at any level.

MAINTENANCE TECHNICIAN

The maintenance technician is charged with keeping the machinery in optimum condition. It is also his or her job to keep records and to note any problems before they develop into major headaches. For instance, everyone knows that oil changes are necessary for maintenance, whether it's a truck or the family car. However, a sharp maintenance technician can spot some problems in the development stage by studying the used oil during an oil change. In fact, the industry now relies on high-tech equipment to test used oil to ascertain ring and bearing wear, fuel inconsistencies, and a dozen other problems that are apparent from the aroma, consistency, and quality of used oil as it is drained from the vehicle.

In simpler times, a maintenance technician was trained in-house and gradually worked from a trainee position to maintenance and, eventually, to mechanic. Due to the high-tech nature of the business, this practice is beginning to disappear and be replaced by trained technicians from vocational-technical schools who are further trained, oftentimes, in specialized schools run by engine manufacturers such as Cummins or Detroit.

Maintenance includes far more than just the engine. It includes every item on the vehicle, from signal lights to wheel lugs. Each repair that has to be made on the road costs the company time, wages, and money, and companies depend on their maintenance teams to prevent these costly breakdowns. It is vital to the company's bottom line of profit to ensure that their vehicles leave the terminal not only in optimum mechanical shape, but also in condition to pass the various DOT and ICC requirements the state and federal governments impose.

Surprise vehicle inspections at weigh stations and checkpoints across the country are becoming increasingly common. While it falls to the safety person to make sure both driver and vehicle meet the safety standards of the area where the rig operates, it is the maintenance person's responsibility to make sure that the vehicle itself is fully operational and safe to send out onto the road.

MECHANIC

In addition to the maintenance technician, there is a second type of maintenance person. This is the full-fledged truck mechanic who is capable of tearing down an engine or transmission, repairing or rebuilding it, and getting the rig back in shape to hit the road once more. As mentioned earlier, vehicles are getting more complicated each year, and many companies have moved away from an in-house, full-service repair shop. The cost of purchasing the new high-tech testing equipment—much of which now requires computer knowledge—and the cost of training fully certified mechanics as new innovations hit the market can be very high.

However, even as equipment costs continue to climb, there is some evidence of a comeback of the fully rated truck mechanic. Not every company can justify the $100,000-plus outlay for a new truck and trailer every few years. These operations require considerably more than a general maintenance technician. Yet, no one starts out as a fully qualified mechanic, and one of the best routes to attaining this level is by beginning as a maintenance person and working up from there. Thus a trained mechanic is valuable both for his or her own work and as someone who can train the rest of the maintenance staff.

EARNINGS AND TRAINING

Wages are, at the very least, interesting in the maintenance area. They range from a paltry $7 an hour for an absolute untrained beginner to figures approaching $65,000 for shop foremen in major operations. And maintenance is one field where there will always be a demand for workers.

Today's trucking operations seem to prefer to hire their maintenance people from vocational-technical trade schools. The reasoning is that these students have at least a rudimentary grounding in the basic skills required to perform maintenance on trucks. It is common for companies to invest a great deal of money in tuition for specialized courses to get their maintenance staff certified and trained. Courses range from TIG welding to original engine manufacturing classes.

Visit any full-service truck shop today and you will more than likely see various diplomas and certificates framed and displayed on the office walls. Many companies do not see additional training as an expense, but as an investment. Of course, company sponsored training is an obvious way to learn the ropes and gain valuable hands-on experience if you want to eventually own your own business.

DRAWBACKS

Like most work, maintenance is a job with some drawbacks. Obviously, you may face hard physical demands with the job. It's one of the few areas of trucking where muscle is sometimes required. It can also be a high-pressure occupation. Very often, a tractor or trailer will stop at the shop en route and loaded. Suddenly you'll find yourself working under a tight deadline to get a rig road-ready and back under a load within a matter of hours. It's not at all unusual to see an impatient driver pacing up and down a waiting area waiting for maintenance to finish with the truck so he or she can get back on the road and earn a living.

And, as you might guess, maintenance is not a job for people who dislike getting their hands dirty. Trucks ooze, seep, leak, drip, and dribble, and the older a unit becomes, the more common this behavior seems. You'll also find drivers who take care of their truck like it was one of their own children, and others who will make you seethe because their rig will exhibit half a dozen problems that could have been fixed or prevented if the driver had only taken a second to check the vehicle. Frustration comes with the territory.

A TYPICAL DAY'S WORK

To gain an idea of what maintenance entails, let's take a look at some of the routine tasks a mechanic might encounter on any given day working for a company with leased vehicles or trucks under extended warranty.

As the trucks come in from the road, they are checked into maintenance, and generally the driver is asked to complete an inspection or "gripe" sheet. It is, in fact, a list of items that the driver knows need attention. One of the most common "gripes" is "vibration," which is often a case of misaligned or unbalanced wheels, but can be caused by a number of other things, like a bearing going bad in the drive shaft, uneven tire wear, or an imbalance in fuel distribution causing uneven firing within the cylinders. Drivers tend to have an aversion to paperwork, and it can be something of a challenge to figure out what a driver means by, "It makes a funny noise in third gear," or some equally cryptic comment. Often a maintenance technician must interview the driver to obtain details. In short, the technician becomes a detective.

Trucks do vibrate. It's a fact of life, and most operate in excess of 100,000 miles each year. This translates to more than 2,000 hours of operation, which means that everything from mirror mounts to suspension parts are subjected to a constant vibration. This, in turn, tends to cause things to loosen or wear. Although drivers perform a pretrip inspection, it is not as detailed as the inspection maintenance personnel must make. Something as simple as a loose mirror bracket is, at the very least, irksome and, at worst, a major safety hazard.

The average truck/trailer combination has about 31 lights, ranging from signal lights to marker lamps. One manufacturer claims that the average road unit contains as much as 22 miles of wire, all of it subject to the rigors of that 2,000 hours of road operation. The electrical system is one of the first areas a maintenance technician will check. It is also, almost all maintenance people agree, one of the most exasperating systems to service and repair. Finding a short or a loose connection in that huge mass of wire can represent a major challenge, especially if an amateur mechanic has been working on it before and jury-rigged the system to make it function.

Unfortunately, the electrical system is also an area that DOT inspectors always check during vehicle inspections. A faulty signal or marker can translate into hundreds of dollars in fines, a half-day delay on the road, and the cost of an overpriced roadside service call. To the company, this expense is a bit extreme when something as simple as a loose connection or a burned out bulb may have caused the problem.

As the trucks are checked in, the maintenance foreman or shop foreman will assign a technician to the vehicle and supply him or her with a list of possible problems. There is often a checklist of regular maintenance routines included with the "problem" list, and the technician's job is to go over both lists thoroughly and carefully, repairing or replacing items as necessary. In some of the bigger operations, maintenance technicians specialize, with one handling electrical work; another servicing wheels, bearings, and tires, and so on. In other operations, one technician is assigned one truck and will work on that unit until all the problems are resolved.

Keeping Records

As repairs are made, each part and each labor or test performed is recorded. This is vital for a number of reasons. First, it helps the shop parts room keep track of inventory and lets them know when it's time to reorder standard stock items. These records also tell the chief of maintenance where a truck stands in its maintenance schedule. The chief must see to it that regular maintenance activities, such as oil changes and tire rotations, take place according to this pre-set schedule. For trucks operating under warranty, this schedule is vital because most warranties are void if routine and regular maintenance is not performed on the vehicle. Maintenance records also inform the chief if a vehicle is showing premature wear, which gives the mechanics a chance to correct the problem before it becomes worse. Premature wear may be a maintenance problem or may indicate a problem with the assigned driver of the vehicle.

Often the head of the maintenance department will receive related information on the unit from bookkeeping, or from wherever records are maintained concerning mileage and fuel consumption. If a truck shows too much fuel usage compared to the rest of the fleet, either it has a mechanical problem, usually within the fuel pump or injection system, or the driver is not operating the vehicle in an economical way and may need to receive a reprimand or specific instructions to rectify the situation. If it's a mechanical problem, and if the company has a policy of rewarding thrifty drivers with fuel bonuses, this aspect of maintenance takes on an even bigger importance. Without it, the company is not fairly compensating the driver of a faulty truck.

New and Used Trucks

Maintenance works with a number of other departments within the company and may also cooperate with businesses outside the immediate company. For instance, the maintenance shop people are constantly on the lookout for bargains for the standard maintenance parts, such as filters or oil. In addition, maintenance almost always reports to purchasing as trucks enter and leave the shop. Mileage and maintenance records are passed on to the purchasing department and are used to make decisions about when to sell off a truck from the fleet and replace it with a new one. For many companies, this decision is based on a preset number of miles—usually 350,000 to one million—when they feel the truck's dependability may be decreasing and the cost of major maintenance and repairs on the truck is a less sound investment than replacing the vehicle with a new one.

Again, here is a primary reason to maintain and compile accurate and thorough records on a vehicle. To the purchaser of a used truck, vehicle mileage is less important than the availability of shop records. These records indicate not only what has been done to the vehicle over its lifetime, but what hasn't been done, which often is more significant than what repairs have taken place recently. For instance, a tractor may have 500,000 miles—a figure that is only middle-aged for a truck—but if it has never had an in-frame engine overhaul, the truck will need this expensive type of service sometime soon. For a buyer, this makes a major difference in what he or she may be willing to pay for the vehicle.

In some companies, the disposition of the used vehicles involves a direct link between driver and maintenance. Many companies offer in-house purchasing programs to their drivers. For many operations, this system has proved an expedient and profitable way to remove an older truck from the fleet and, at the same time, help a driver move from the status of a company driver to an owner/operator. It also has the secondary, but no less important, effect of making it more likely that a driver will stay with the company—first because of the opportunity for ownership, and later because the company is financing the used tractor for the driver. In-house purchasing programs are an effective driver retention tool, but only if the trucks are maintained adequately so that drivers know they can depend on their equipment. Very often—almost always, in fact—these drivers will continue to have their trucks maintained in the company shop. In fact, some sales contracts require it.

This requirement may sound a bit like a monopoly, but often it is for both the driver's and the company's protection. Maintenance will perform the same checks and service on the privately owned vehicle as they do on the company rigs. The difference is that these services are charged to the driver, but usually at a reduced rate compared to a standard truck shop.

CHAPTER 11

COMPANY WATCHDOG

It's been called the least popular position in the trucking industry, yet it is one of the most vital. The *safety person* is, in effect, the company cop. He or she must see to it that every truck and every driver in the firm remains within the boundaries of safe operation and of the law of each state where the rig operates. It's much easier to describe than to accomplish.

LOG BOOKS

Paperwork is one of the safety person's major responsibilities. The law requires drivers to file and maintain current log books whenever they are on duty. These log books must comply with federally mandated standards, up to and including the fact that they must be filled out in ink. The safety department checks the logs of each driver to make sure they are, first of all, filled out correctly. Here, little things count. The driver must use his or her full name on the log sheet, must maintain a daily accumulated hours chart, must show loading and unloading periods. If the driver was stopped at a weigh station for a DOT inspection, that, too, must be noted in the log book.

To give an idea of just how much importance is placed on these records, records must be retained for six months, and the Department of Transportation has audit rights to ensure the compliance of the company. Carriers can be fined thousands of dollars for hours-of-service violations.

More than money can be at stake, and once again, the topic of the use of computers arises. In 1996, seven employees of a major Iowa trucking company found themselves on the way to federal prison for falisification of logs. In part, this was due to on-board computer records from the rigs, which in no way agreed with the recorded hard copy of logs the company maintained in its files. While this was an isolated instance, and the circumstances of falsification were quite blatant, the incident should serve as a warning. Moreover, most experts agree that on-board computers are the wave of the future—eventually to become a requirement rather than an option.

It is the safety officer's job to ensure that logs are accurate and up-to-date. The penalties for failure, as you can see, can be quite extreme.

Perhaps this emphasis on detail sounds like nit-picking. In a sense, it is. Yet, like the weather, it does no good whatsoever to argue about these rules; it is unlikely that they will change dramatically. In 1951 many truck lines were taking out full-page ads in newspapers and magazines decrying the rules and regulations placed upon them. It may have gained them a little public sympathy for a while, but little else.

Those rules are still on the book, along with dozens of others. And it is the safety person's job to see to it that these rules are followed.

THE DRIVER'S ADVOCATE

Most safety people were drivers at one time or another. This makes the job somewhat simpler since one part of most safety positions is testing potential drivers, both by written exam and by a driving exam. Perhaps it sounds as though the safety department is the driver's enemy. This is untrue. In fact, it can be the driver's best friend.

For example, one of the most common errors that can be committed in the industry is to exceed the hours of service. Often, this happens when dispatch sends a truck from Point A to Point B on an unreasonable schedule. If you have a load that needs to travel fifteen hundred miles, and you only have 24 hours to make delivery, you cannot possibly make that run in a legal manner. It is the dispatcher's job to see that loads are dispatched and moved on a workable schedule, but sometimes they exceed the parameters of safety and good sense in performing their duties. This places the driver in an extremely awkward position. On the one hand, he or she has a load that dispatch says must absolutely, positively be in the shipper's hands no later than noon the next day. On the other hand, the driver faces the very real risk of running afoul of the law by spending too many hours on duty to get the load delivered at the time the dispatch department is demanding. As a driver, if you violate the laws governing hours of service, *the fine is yours.* Big deal? In states like California, the fine may amount to as much as $500 or $600! Few, if any, companies will pay a fine for this type of violation. Moreover, you will, in all likelihood, be held for eight hours at the weigh station where you were caught in violation, until the required hours of off-duty service are met.

A smart driver caught in this position will call his or her safety department and explain the situation. Safety, in turn, will contact dispatch and tell them in no uncertain terms what the law says. In fact, the safety department will force dispatch to reschedule the load to fall within legal time slots. No legitimate company forces its drivers to violate the law, though at one time this was a very common practice.

ACCIDENT PREVENTION

Perhaps is sounds as though too much emphasis is placed upon such things as log books and hours of service. More than one planner, dispatcher, marketing rep, or driver has argued with a tough, efficient safety department over "silly" rules like hours of service. Yet, more than one safety person has had to read an accident report that contained these words: "...fell asleep at the wheel." The safety department is charged with protecting the driver, the load, the equipment, and the motoring public. And accidents *do* happen.

In 1975, a truck driver pulled off the side of a major four-lane highway when he began to get sleepy. He left his marker lights on and was completely off the traveled portion of the highway and clearly visible. A husband and wife, returning from a party, both with blood-alcohol levels far above the legal limits, slammed into the back of the trailer and were killed instantly. The family of the couple sued.

In court, the trucking company proved that the couple was undoubtedly legally drunk based on evidence from the coroner's report and from eyewitness accounts of the couple's erratic driving prior to the accident. The couple was traveling well in excess of the legal speed limit, and they rammed the truck without any apparent attempt to slow or brake their car, even though the trailer was lighted and clearly visible.

Who was at fault?

The answer is shocking. The truck driver and his company were sued for over a million dollars! How and why? It is illegal to park a truck on the shoulder of a roadway except in an emergency, and then markers or flares must be set out in accordance with DOT safety standards. It is the safety department's duty to see to it that their drivers are fully aware of the rules, laws, and regulations pertaining to safe operation of a commercial vehicle so that accidents like this one can be avoided.

MEETING STATE AND FEDERAL STANDARDS

In 1990, safety departments were faced with a changing set of rules and regulations that reshaped the industry. One of the most noticeable were the new laws governing drivers' licensing and mandatory drug tests. Like their law enforcement counterparts, safety people monitor driving records and driver safety violations. In most companies, "points" accrue for serious safety violations. If a driver accumulates too many points, he or she is either suspended or terminated. In today's industry, one drug violation is grounds for termination. Drug tests are now mandatory. Moreover, most major companies also test drivers randomly, without announcing the test ahead of time. If the company's safety department is found negligent in testing, the entire company may be fined heavily, or even shut down until a complete overhaul of safety procedures is implemented. The amount of revenue lost from a federal DOT shutdown is staggering.

In Minnesota, a routine DOT surprise inspection of a major company's drivers' logs netted 52 violations in the first 100 logs reviewed. The DOT gave a written warning to the company to get their "act" in order. Two months later, DOT again inspected the logs, pulling 100 samples at random. Once again, more than half were found to be in violation. The company was shut down for three full working days, which meant that trucks, drivers, and loads were marooned all over the country while the safety staff desperately worked to get their department up to snuff. The results were a hefty fine from the federal DOT, an increase in spot checks of the company's trucks and drivers by officials at weigh stations across the country, and monthly inspections by DOT officials. These penalties amounted to revenue losses of more than half a million dollars during the three-day shutdown, plus the loss of customer confidence from the shutdown.

The safety department is charged with seeing that the driver and his or her equipment remain in constant compliance with both state and federal mandates. Regulations require that all drivers submit a detailed resume of all commercial driving experience up to 10 years back and that their operator's permit be run through the department of motor vehicles computer background check. Additional requirements for drivers include an annual statement of moving violations and annual DOT physicals—usually at company expense after the initial physical. All drivers must be able to present up-to-date physical cards. The safety department also works with accident investigations and studies, keeps track of driver violations, and works with the maintenance department to see that every truck in the fleet is well within the guidelines set forth both by federal law and manufacturer specifications.

ADDITIONAL DUTIES

In most companies, the safety department is also in charge of all driver training. Many companies require their drivers to attend refresher courses in safety procedures even though a driver may be very experienced. These courses review everything from the pretrip vehicle inspection to the steps drivers should take if they are involved in an accident.

Most safety personnel work closely with other divisions within the company, especially claims, personnel, and maintenance. Often, safety departments work with organizations outside the trucking operation as well. This includes insurance companies and law enforcement agencies. It is a job that is sometimes thankless because, from time to time, rules and regulations conflict with the conduct of day-to-day business. Yet, a strong safety department is absolutely vital to the success of the company.

At times, the safety department is expected to make suggestions on how safety can be improved based on its studies of the business operation. In the case of one midwestern hauler, the safety study revealed that almost all traffic accidents happened to their drivers between the hours of midnight and 5 A.M. In response, the company created a policy that all vehicles must shut down no later than midnight. Violations of the policy would result in driver termination. The end result was a marked reduction in accidents.

However, the safety department is not all-powerful. The same company that implemented the rules concerning shut down between midnight and 5 A.M. is again running round the clock. Why? There was so much pressure from the marketing department and from their shippers that the safety procedure was overridden and the company returned to their original methods of travel and dispatch...and accidents again went up. Safety can be a very frustrating business when it collides with the financial bottom line.

The safety department also offers driver incentives—safety bonuses. Monetary rewards and safety awards are based on records maintained by the safety department. Many companies believe that drivers should not only be penalized for unsafe operation, but rewarded when they display a consistent track record of safe driving. In the past, competitions between companies have actually sprung up to see who could compile the highest number of nonviolation miles.

Some companies actually place safety spotters on the highway. Although it may sound a bit "big-brotherish," these spotters follow the routes their company drivers travel and will, from time to time, stop the drivers and do a routine safety check on everything from paperwork to equipment. These safety checks are unpopular with the drivers, but many operations claim that incidents of log violations, traffic citations, and accidents have been reduced by the presence of company spotters.

EARNINGS

Wages for a safety person vary widely, depending on their responsibilities and the size of the company. A seasoned safety person with a major company can expect wages well in excess of $30,000. In major fleets, safety directors often earn over $50,000, though this never happens overnight. In small companies, safety is often an additional task for the office secretary or bookkeeper and wages are considerably lower.

Careers in safety outside the trucking industry include law enforcement, working for the federal or state DOT, and similar positions. Any business that is subject to safety regulations can be a career choice for a safety person.

CHAPTER 12

OR YOU MIGHT CONSIDER...

PAYROLL

Nobody works for free. And, as we have already seen, payment within the industry can be very complicated, especially for marketing people and for drivers. So, as you might imagine, a person who works in payroll or bookkeeping must have excellent math skills.

Even for those who are well qualified, doing payroll for a trucking company is a tough job. The industry has some wrinkles that other businesses don't and that can make the job an extreme challenge. For instance, in the late 1970s during the fuel crisis and prior to deregulation, trucking rates were still frozen. When the price of diesel fuel went from 19 cents per gallon to a dollar per gallon, the change raised havoc within the industry, and it forced some companies out of business.

Eventually, the federal government stepped in and introduced the federal fuel surcharge, which was levied against certain types of commodities and hauling. The surcharge was a percentage based on the average fuel price, and it changed from week to week. For drivers paid on percentage—for contract drivers and owner/operators leased to carriers—it meant their checks might include a 4 percent surcharge one week and a 6 percent surcharge the next. Payroll and book-keeping had to check hauling dates, log books, and all sorts of information before payroll checks could be cut. These were the days when the lights burned late in the windows of many trucking offices across the country.

In addition to handling regular paychecks, another major function of the payroll department is advances. It is standard policy for most companies to supply cash advances to their drivers on the road. This may be done in a number of ways, ranging from a company credit card for fuel purchases only to a system of "instant" checks that are issued via a code when the driver calls in and requests more operating capital. Most companies have a set policy on how much money driv-ers can draw in a given time period, or against their load. Often someone in payroll is responsible for issuing these advances and for keeping track of them.

Working in the offices of a trucking company can be a fast-paced experience. There are order writers, switchboard operators, and the usual assortment of file clerks and secre-taries. In addition, larger companies have a position that is rapidly growing in importance as the driver shortage grows more acute: recruiters.

RECRUITERS AND INSTRUCTORS

Recruiters do exactly what their name implies; they recruit new people to the company. At times, and in some operations, they may never leave the office. Or, they may travel constantly, attending career days at community colleges or visiting with driving schools across the country. Usually, the recruiter is the first person you talk to when you contact the company, and most will act as a guide for you as you reach a career decision and begin the long process of interviews, paperwork, and tests. In a sense, the recruiter is the public relations arm of the industry, and many of the top recruiters come from other divisions of the business, including driving.

Some trucking companies entrust the recruiters with contractual negotiations with driving schools and drivers. Many schools are contracted to carriers, and the recruiter is something of a go-between between the company and the school. It is very likely that the paperwork you fill out when you enter a driving school will be scrutinized by a recruiter, and it's equally possible that your progress as you move through the school will be monitored as well.

Other positions exist in companies that perform some or all of their own training in-house. Instructors are hired to teach students everything from how to back a trailer to how to operate the load locks to how to spot a potential claim. Some companies even have a group of drivers who will run first-seat of a team operation with a new driver the first few times he or she is dispatched out, just to see that beginners learn the proper techniques.

HIGH-TECH INNOVATIONS

As the world of computers invades the workplace, the trucking industry is rapidly taking advantage of new innovations and ideas. Computer programmers and operators are always in demand, and more and more companies are moving into specialized computer applications that call for highly trained people.

For example, systems now exist that allow companies to track and locate individual loads through a network of satellite uplinks. These systems are so accurate that they can pinpoint a truck's location within a hundred feet. In addition, for refrigerated loads, the computer operator can adjust the refrigeration unit's temperature setting, check oil and fluid levels, monitor load temperatures and engine temperatures, implement two-way communication with the driver, and even ascertain whether the trailer doors are open or closed. The system works something like the LORAN radio location system used for airline navigation, and it can even be used to detect theft. Obviously, it takes a skilled computer operator to work the system.

Another innovation is the custom designed voice mail—another computerized system—that cures the old headache a driver and dispatcher often had of being unable to reach each other during peak phone traffic periods. It's basically a private recorded number assigned to each driver—usually by truck or employee number. The system is programmed so that the driver may call in to receive messages—such as where to pick up the next load—or the driver can send messages—such as notifying dispatch that he or she is empty or running late. In larger companies on-board computers, fax machines, direct keyboard communication, cell phones, and more are becoming the rule rather than the exception. Skilled workers are needed to run the computers and maintain these systems.

WAREHOUSE

A great many companies maintain their own warehousing systems. The way most systems work is that a local truck will pick up a shipment, or part of a shipment, bring it to the terminal and drop it at the company warehouse. It is held there until an over-the-road truck is empty and ready to roll again, then the shipment is reloaded into the trailer and sent on its way. Warehouse workers, forklift operators, and billing specialists are all needed to maintain the efficiency of this type of operation. Just keeping track of what comes in and what leaves can be a major headache, and, in a larger operation, there may be a dozen trucks loading and unloading at once. Inventory and control become a major concern in this type of atmosphere.

It should be noted that if you are interested in the driving end of the trucking business, but are not yet old enough to become a driver, the warehouse is one of the best and easiest places to begin your career. Here you'll get an idea of what the drivers haul, how it's hauled, and whether trucking is really what you want to do for a living.

OTHER SPECIALIZATIONS

Another specialized area within larger companies is the retrieval of equipment or cargo after breakdowns or accidents. Major fleets often maintain their own minifleet of vehicles and specially trained teams to handle accidents or breakdowns. These teams drive to the site and either retrieve the salvage or drop off a replacement vehicle, and they tow the disabled truck back to the terminal for repair.

Finally, there is the position of buyer. Major haulers set up contracts across the country for everything from fuel to tires. As the market changes, it is someone's responsibility to see to it that the company obtains the best price possible. The savings of one or two cents a gallon for fuel alone can amount to tens of thousands of dollars for a major carrier. Buyers will also set up fleet maintenance contracts in areas where they do not maintain a terminal to handle breakdowns, tire repairs, or even something as simple as a truck wash. Being a buyer may sound a bit like a professional shopper's job, but it takes a great deal of business savvy to compile the best overall deals.

Whatever position you select in the trucking industry, the challenges and rewards will be great. The business offers endless possibilities, and new recruits are needed every day!

PROFESSIONAL ASSOCIATIONS AND ORGANIZATIONS

American Moving and Storage Association
1611 Duke Street
Alexandria, VA 22314
(708) 638-7410

American Public Transit Association
1201 New York Avenue, N.W., #400
Washington, DC 20005
(202) 898-4000

American Truck Dealers
8400 Westpark Drive
McLean, VA 22102
(703) 821-7116
(800) 252-6232

American Truck Historical Society
300 Office Park Drive
No. 120
Birmingham, AL 35223
(205) 870-0566

American Truck Stop Foundation
1199 N. Fairfax Street
Suite 801
Alexandria, VA 22314
(703) 549-2100

American Truck Stop Owners Association
P.O. Box 4949
Winston-Salem, NC 27115-4949
(910) 744-5555

American Trucking Association
2200 Mill Road
Alexandria, VA 22314-4677
(703) 838-1700
(800) ATA-LINE

Americans for Safe and Competitive Trucking
314 Massachusetts Avenue
Washington, DC 20002
(205) 544-5030

**Bureau of Transportation
Statistics**
400 7th Street, S.W.
Room 3430
Washington, DC 20590
(202) 366-DATA

**Commission of Accredited
Truck Driving Schools**
1725 Duke Street
Suite 600
Alexandria, VA 22314-3457
(703) 549-0124

**Distribution and LTL Carriers
Association**
211 N. Union Street
Suite 102
Alexandria, VA
22314
(703) 739-3101

**Federal Highway
Administration**
400 7th Street, S.W.
Washington, DC 20590
(202) 366-0660

**Federal Transit
Administration**
400 7th Street,
S.W.
Washington, DC 20590
(202) 366-4319

**Independent Truckers and
Drivers Association**
1109 Plover Drive
Baltimore, MD 21227
(410) 242-0507

**Intermodal Association of North
America**
7501 Greenway Center Drive
Suite 720
Greenbelt, MD 20770-3514
(301) 982-3400

International Road Federation
2600 Virginia Avenue, N.W.
Suite 208
Washington, DC 20037
(202) 338-4641

**International Tire and Rubber
Association**
P.O. Box 37203
Louisville, KY 40233-7203
(502) 968-8900

**Institute of Transportation
Engineers**
525 School Street, S.W.
Suite 410
Washington, DC 20024-2797
(202) 554-8050

Mid-West Truckers Association
2727 N. Dirksen Parkway
Springfield, IL 62702
(217) 525-0310

NATSO, Inc.
(formerly the National
Association of Truck
Stop Operators)
1199 N. Fairfax Street
Suite 801
Alexandria, VA 22314
(703) 549-2100

National Association of Trailer Manufacturers
3310 S.W. Harrison Street
Topeka, KS 66611
(913) 266-7014

National Customs Brokers and Forwarders Association of America
1200 18th Street, N.W.
Suite 901
Washington, DC 20036
(202) 466-0222

National Highway Traffic Safety Administration
400 7th Street, S.W., #5232
Washington, DC 20590
(202) 366-9550
(800) 424-9393

National Industrial Transportation League
1700 N. Moore Street
Suite 1900
Arlington, VA 22209-1904
(703) 524-5011

National Private Truck Council
66 Canal Center Plaza
Suite 600
Alexandria, VA 22314
(703) 683-1300

National Safety Council
1121 Spring Lake Drive
Itasca, IL 60143
(630) 285-1121

National Tank Truck Carriers
2200 Mill Road
Alexandria, VA 22314
(703) 838-1960

North American Transportation Management Institute
2200 Mill Road
Alexandria, VA 22314
(703) 838-7952

Owner-Operator Independent Drivers Association
P.O. Box L
Grain Valley, MO 64029
(816) 229-5791
(800) 444-5791

Professional Truck Drivers Institute of America
2200 Mill Road
Alexandria, VA 22314
(703) 838-8842

Professional Trucking Services Association
United Truckers Service
1385 Iris Drive
Conyers, GA 30208
(770) 922-6200

Society of Automotive Engineers
400 Commonwealth Drive
Warrendale, PA 15096-0001
(412) 776-4841

Society of Professional Drivers
P.O. Box 491
Paoli, PA 19301
(610) 647-0818

Specialized Carriers & Rigging Association
2750 Prosperity Avenue
Suite 620
Fairfax, VA 22031-4312
(703) 698-0291

Transportation Research Board
2101 Constitution Avenue, N.W.
Washington, DC 20418
(202) 334-2934

Transportation Research Forum
11250 Roger Bacon Drive
Suite 8
Reston, VA 20190
(703) 437-4377

Truck Manufacturers Association
1225 New York Avenue, N.W.
Suite 300
Washington, DC 20005-6156
(202) 638-7825

Truck Renting and Leasing Association
1725 Duke Street
Suite 600
Alexandria, VA 22314
(703) 299-9120

Truck Trailer Manufacturers Association
1020 Princess Street
Alexandria, VA 22314
(703) 549-3010

Truck Writers of North America
600 Reisterstown Road
Suite 404
Baltimore, MD 21208
(410) 486-7430

Trucking Management, Inc.
2233 Wisconsin Avenue, N.W.
Washington, DC 20007
(202) 965-7660

Truckload Carriers Association
2200 Mill Road
3rd Floor
Alexandria, VA 22314
(703) 838-1950

U.S. Department of Transportation
400 7th Street, S.W.
Washington, DC 20590
(202) 366-5580

BIBLIOGRAPHY

PERIODICALS

Allied News (quarterly)
1199 N. Fairfax Street
Suite 801
Alexandria, VA 22314
(703) 549-2100

American Truck Dealer (monthly)
8400 Westpark Drive
McLean, VA 22102
(703) 821-7116
(800) 252-6232

American Trucking Trends
(annual)
2200 Mill Road
Alexandria, VA 22314-4677
(703) 838-1700
(800) ATA-LINE

Canadian Shipper (bimonthly)
Kenilworth Publishing Inc.
500 Cochrane Drive
Unit 5
Markham, ON
L3R 8F2
Canada

Canadian Transportation
(monthly)
Southam Communications, Ltd.
1450 Don Mills Road
Don Mill, ON
M3B 2X7
Canada

Commercial Carrier Journal
(monthly)
Chilton Company
Chilton Way
Radnor, PA 19089

Fleet Owner (monthly)
FM Business Publications, Inc.
475 Park Avenue South
New York, NY 10016

Guardrail (monthly)
2200 Mill Road
Alexandria, VA 22314
(703) 838-7952

*Heavy Duty Trucking: The
    Business Magazine of
    Trucking* (monthly)
1800 E. Deere Avenue
Santa Ana, CA 92705

Keep on Truckin' News (monthly)
2727 N. Dirksen Parkway
Springfield, IL 62702
(217) 525-0310

Land Line (monthly)
P.O. Box L
Grain Valley, MO 64029
(816) 229-5791
(800) 444-5791

*Logistics and Transportation
    Review* (quarterly)
Faculty of Commerce
University of British Columbia
Vancouver, BC
V6T 1W5
Canada

*Overdrive: The Magazine for the
    American Trucker* (monthly)
Overdrive Magazine, Inc.
P.O. Box 3187
Tuscaloosa, AL 35403

Private Carrier (monthly)
1320 Braddock Plaza
Suite 720
Alexandria, VA 22314
(703) 683-1300

*Transport Topics: National
    Newspaper of the Trucking
    Industry* (weekly)
American Trucking
    Associations
2200 Mill Road
Alexandria, VA 22314-9972

Transportation and Distribution
    (monthly)
Pewton Publications
1100 Superior Avenue
Cleveland, OH 44114-2543

Truckers Newsletter (monthly)
1109 Plover Drive
Baltimore, MD 21227
(410) 242-0507

World Highways (8 times/year)
2600 Virginia Avenue, N.W.
Suite 208
Washington, DC 20037
(202) 338-4641

BOOKS

American Trade Schools Directory. Jericho, N.Y.: Croner Publications, Inc., 1991.

American Trucking Associations. *Truck Driver Handbook.* Alexandria, Va.: American Trucking Associations, 1994.

Begun, Abbey, Mark Siegel, and Nancy Jacobs. *Transportation—America's Lifeline.* Wylie, Tex.: Information Plus, 1997.

Grill, Lewis. *Introduction to Heavy Duty Trucking: A Preparation Text for Entry-Level Drivers.* Billings, Mont.: Atlantic Pacific Resource Group, 1993.

Gunnell, John. *Trucking in America: Moving the Goods.* Iola, Wis.: Krause Publications, Inc., 1995.

Ingram, Arthur and Martin Phippard. *Highway Heavy Metal.* Poole, Eng.: Blandford Press, 1986.

Kowalke, Ron. *Trucking in America: Moving the Goods.* Iola, Wis.: Krause Publications, 1995.

Lewis, Jerre G. and Renn, Leslie D. *How to Start & Manage an Independent Trucking Business: Step-by-Step Guide to Business Success.* Interlochen, Mich.: Lewis & Renn Associates, 1995.

Ouellet, Lawrence J. *Pedal to the Metal—The Work Lives of Truckers.* Philadelphia: Temple University Press, 1994.

Riemer, Otto. *Journal of a Trucker.* Galesville, Wis.: O. Riemer, 1995.

Rothe, J. Peter. *The Trucker's World: Risk, Safety & Mobility.* New Brunswick, N.J.: Transaction Publications, 1991.

Russell, William. *Truckers.* Vero Beach, Fla.: Rourke Publishing Group, 1994.

Saccomanno, F. Frank and Shortreed, J.H. *Truck Safety: Perceptions and Reality.* Waterloo, Ont.: Institute for Risk Research, University of Waterloo, 1996.

Schauer, Donald D. *Careers in Trucking.* New York: Rosen Publishing Group, 1991.

Terebecki, M.K. *The Vanishing Trucking Pioneers.* Marietta, Ga.:Pioneer Press, 1990.

Teske, Paul Eric. *Deregulating Freight Transportation: Delivering the Goods.* Washington, D.C.: AEI Press, 1995.

Ware, John H. *Discover the World of Trucking.* Chapel Hill, N.C.: Professional Pr., 1993.

Will, Frederic. *Big Rig Souls: Truckers in America's Heartland.* West Bloomfield, Mich.: A&M, 1992.

SELECTED LIST OF PRIVATE TRUCK DRIVING SCHOOLS

This is a selected list of private truck driving schools in the United States and Canada. Consult *American Trade Schools Directory* (updated looseleaf service, See Appendix B) for state listings of vocational-technical schools and community colleges that offer truck driving courses in the United States and Puerto Rico. This publication is available in school counselor offices and public libraries.

UNITED STATES

America's Driving Force
P.O. Box 16845
Atlanta, GA 30321
(404) 608-8608

Diesel Institute of America
P.O. Box 69
Gainesville, MD 21536
(800) 638-5490

and

4710 E. 7th Avenue
Tampa, FL 33605
(800) 572-4327

FleetSafe Corporation
448 E. Paces Ferry Road
Atlanta, GA 30305
(800) 800-8096

Georgia Driving Academy
1449 VFW Drive
Conyers, GA 30207
(770) 918-8501
(800) 711-4301

J&B Trucking Training Center
108 W. Van Emmon Street
P.O. Box 194
Yorkville, IL 60568
(630) 553-9009
(800) 300-9983

MTA Commercial Driving Schools
4101 Oates Road
Houston, TX 77013
(800) 304-8857

and

600 Cinderlane Parkway
Orlando, FL 32810
(800) 346-5820
call (800) 452-3629 for
additional locations

National Truck Drivers School
188 College Drive
P.O. Box 1899
Orange Park, FL 32067
(800) 488-SEMI

National Truck Driving School
9600 E. 104th Avenue
Henderson, CO 80640
(303) 288-2228
(800) 829-7364

Smith & Solomon Truck and Bus
Driving Schools
45 Kilmer Road
Edison, NJ 08817
(800) 622-0355

and

721 Cuthbert Boulevard
Cherry Hill, NJ 08000
(800) 253-0467

and

2011 Woodhaven Road
Philadelphia, PA 19100
(888) 417-5484

Tri-State Semi Driver Training
6690 Germantown Road
Middletown, OH 45042
(800) 860-7364

Western Pacific Truck School
435 W. Benjamin Holt Drive
Stockton, CA 95207
(209) 472-1500
(800) 333-1233

Winsor's Tractor Trailer Driving
School
3106 Southwood Avenue
Linden, NJ 07036
(800) 795-5501

CANADA

Atlantic Transport Training
    Academy
P.O. Box 90
George Street
Apohaqui, NB
EOG 1A0
Canada
(506) 432-4913
(800) 563-8782

5th Wheel Training Institute
536 Brazeau Boulevard
Dymond Industrial Road
P.O. Box 1345
New Liskeard, ON
P0J 1P0
Canada

Tri-County Truck Driver Training
2411 Eagle Street North
Cambridge, ON
N3H 4R7
Canada
(519) 653-1700
(800) 265-0400